*

The author: Jean Guitton is a professor
at the Sorbonne in Paris, and a member
of the Academie Française. He is a philosopher and historian of philosophy and
religion, and has published numerous
works in his several fields.

GREAT HERESIES AND CHURCH COUNCILS

GREAT HERESIES
AND CHURCH
COUNCILS

by JEAN GUITTON

HARPER & ROW, PUBLISHERS

New York and Evanston

LIBRARY OF CONGRESS CATALOG CARD NUMBER: 64-20198

TO ROBERT ARON
who made this book come to life

Contents

Introduction

IN 1946, ARNOLD J. TOYNBEE WENT TO PARIS TO LEARN
something about life in France under the occupation. He
visited his friend André Siegfried who said to him: 'All my life
I have studied the history of the 1830, 1848 and 1871 revolutions
in Paris, but I never dared dream that some day I would have
the good fortune to see such things happening under my very
eyes. But then came 1944—and I understood the years 1830,
1848 and 1871 far better than I ever had before. I understood
them because in the year 1944 I myself relived them.'

Just as we are now living, and will in the future be doing so
on a world-wide scale, through an accelerated, *recapitulatory* epoch
of history: an epoch when the ancient phases of human history
will rush past before our eyes (like those films that telescope the
stages of a flower's growth) no longer broken by long intervals,
but following each other in ever faster succession, rushing toward
the better or the worse—toward catastrophe or, alternatively,
toward a new unity of mankind.

In this short volume, the result of reflection, the reader must
not expect to find a résumé, however concise, of the history of
dogma. Unlike the historians whose hard task it is not to skip,
I have selected certain major crises, certain peaks, certain outstanding facts that in my view are charged with significance. I
have studied these events, full of far-reaching consequence, in the
light of the reality of 1963, when the Ecumenical Council is in
suspense; it is to them I have looked for an explanation of the
present interrupted Council, for the meaning, place, and portent
of this Council in universal history. I turn with fear and trembling, and with hope, toward the near and distant future. In
sounding the past, I am trying to sound out the present and the
obscure vision of the future.

The Councils, much though they may differ, can be described
by the same phrase, because they answer the same need: their
purpose is to express the consciousness of the Church, to indicate
her virtualities, her orientations. The Church must define, define
herself—either in answer to a pressing need, an immediate danger,

an imminent crisis, or else in a more natural, more customary manner: simply to fulfil the obligation that rests with every organism—to gain a clearer consciousness of what the whole thinks and believes.

A moment in time turns opaque and illusory if time is arrested, just as a note would in a melody, a syllable in a word, a line in a long poem. Obviously, one would have to stand at the end of time in order to understand the harmony of the entire modulation. But even before that final stop, we can still try to get a view, however obscure, of the direction, the drift, by synthesizing, in writing or description, the history of what went before. Such is the object of this book. Like earlier books, it aims to set out some of what used to be called 'considerations' on the history of Christianity, on the earlier Councils, on the ancient stock-takings of the consciousness of faith.

It is difficult to deal with the history of faith, because one has to adopt an absolute viewpoint. A believer, one who 'has the faith', must introduce into history a privileged axis by which all others will be judged. There will then be various interpretations of the same data. The history of faith written by a Catholic author will be one thing, that written by a Protestant, another.

I cannot escape the responsibility to choose a point of view. I believe one is to be found in all 'histories', even though a false notion of impartiality may prevent its being defined. The political history of France is not the same when written by a monarchist or a democrat, a Christian or a Marxist. Nor need we apologize for this, as though it meant introducing subjectivity into a work of scientific nature. Whenever man gives a recital of man's actions, he brings implicit judgments to bear on the facts, even if only by his omissions and his silences. The only dishonesty in my opinion would be to pretend that man possesses the objectivity of a machine, or to insist that all other historians must now interpret the facts in the same way.

The viewpoint I adopt, because I believe it to be the one which affords the greatest synthesis and is the truest, is that of a Catholic thinker. This short book is not the place for me to set out one by one the divers and converging motives of my choice. I ask the reader to trust me, to refer to my other writings, and to admit for the moment my points of view. If he follows another path, let him make what corrections in emphasis he thinks necessary.

Yet I want to avoid as much as possible the disadvantages that lie in the choice of one single, unique perspective. To do this I shall try to understand as much as it lies in me to do so the other man's position—without, however, justifying it, since that would merely mean that I contradicted myself. In keeping with Catholic usage I am compelled to call 'heresy' the profession of what from the Catholic point of view is not the right opinion—not 'orthodoxy'—and I know full well that others will call my profession 'heresy' from the point of view of their orthodoxy. It goes without saying that when I speak of *heresy* I shall use simply the customary parlance of Catholicism, without attaching the least unkindly meaning to the term. Every one of us could call 'heretics' all those who do not think like him: and, being heretics to one another, we cannot take umbrage at the name. What is needed, what is called for by justice even before it is called for by love, is that we see the promptings and the motives which have led the other person to think as he does, and in this context, led him to cut himself off from the tree of Catholicism.

Whenever the history of belief is written by believers of the various confessions, the *other* doctrine is generally incomprehensible; it falls into what one might call *the mystery of iniquity*. I shall try to avoid giving this distressing impression.

To the unbeliever, theological disputes are empty. They often seem to him a sign of the human mind in decay. He studies these conflicts as he would those relating to mythologies. His lack of understanding makes him incapable of sympathy with the actors and the authors of that history, which he yet claims to be so useful. That sympathy which he finds easy to extend to politicians, soldiers, philosophers, artists, and even mystics (for them he only needs to re-awaken within himself certain latent faculties)—this sympathy he cannot give to theological disputants. For they seem to him to have worked themselves up over concepts that are for him empty of all sense, and to grow all the hotter over minutiæ of definition in proportion as the object of their search has less and less existence; at the end lies logical madness. While the unbeliever can write the history of mysticism, to him strictly

13

a form of religious sentiment, he is ill at ease in the history of dogma, especially when it comes to explaining the various divisions of belief. He states, he copies, he enumerates, he contrasts: but he cannot make us understand the issue, since he himself does not understand it.

Yet we must always recall that the climate in Europe and the West has for twenty centuries remained 'theologico-political', to use Spinoza's term. The whole life of Europe, corner-stone of our planet, is linked up with the Christian orthodoxy, and with the heresies that have torn apart a once coherent form of thought and life, by denying an essential part of that form. Those beliefs are implanted in customs, thoughts, institutions. And the ultimate source of conflicts must be sought in these subterranean motives, man's beliefs. There is no war that is not religious, or as we now say 'ideological'. I am amazed that the study of religious ideas and the study of conflicts have generally been separated, that the history of dogma has been considered useless in the explanation of the great crises of the West.

And so the believer's obligation to have an absolute point of view, and the sceptic's indifference, combine to turn this history of religious thought almost into forbidden territory. That history, the most important history that could be written because it would reach down to deeply hidden springs, touches upon a point within the human mind that is either too greatly irritated, or too blind.

Here I must note a difficulty that arises in any study of heresies undertaken from an absolute viewpoint. And that is that the heresy, like a Platonic idea, seems to have always existed in the realm of shadows and temptations; as though it had come down to earth by settling in an agitated and obstinate brain to become visible among men's minds; if it did have a history before emerging as heterodoxy, it was the clandestine history of all conspiracies; orthodoxy has exposed to the bright light of day a traitor who had always existed in its bosom.

It is difficult to get away from this impression of the virtual existence of the heresies within orthodoxy before their condemnation, difficult not to see in Arius, in Luther, in Pelagius minds which were false from the outset; for the effect of an anathema is

Introduction

to brand the accursed, or rather to create the impression of a prior defect, a black predestination. And every historian tends to make it look as though an event that cannot be explained by its causes could not have been otherwise than it was—that the battle that was won had been won already. In our case, such a false impression is more serious still, since it would lead us to think that there are men who are good, and men who are bad, from the beginning. But the history of the Councils and of condemnations shows how long the Church has hesitated before it did discriminate, and condemn . . .

In the sketches that follow I shall do my utmost, as far as language and the necessity of continuity will allow, to make my readers sense the futures that did not come to be, the oscillations and tremors of the present, and how the 'heretic' might have been orthodox, nay, more: a giant and a saint of orthodoxy; and how, conversely, a Catholic of genius, by an infraction of unity, and by pushing one of his tendencies to the point of folly, might have become a great adversary.

Pascal's image of equilibrium, Bossuet's formula of 'the two ends of the chain' which must be held evenly, are before my mind's eye. Yet I do not think them sufficient: the point is not to hold evenly the two poles of light, and leave what is between them in the shadows, but to see and express how the two truths are to be reconciled with one another. I look on orthodoxy as a structure in full development, a synthesis extremely difficult to define: because it affirms at once both grace and freedom, the authority of the Church and man's inner independence; and in the Eucharist, for example, its character both of a memorial and of reality. These two aspects are not on the same plane:

'Faith embraces several truths that seem to contradict each other.

'The reason for this is the union of the two natures in Jesus Christ.

'There is, then, a large number of truths, of faith as well as morals, that seem mutually repugnant and yet exist together in a wonderful order.

'The source of every heresy lies in not understanding the harmony of the opposing truths, and thinking that they are incompatible . . .

15

'And the source of all the objections the heretics raise against us lies in their not knowing some of our truths.

'And ordinarily it happens that, incapable of understanding the harmony of two opposing truths, and in the belief that to hold one means to exclude the other, they embrace one, exclude the other, and think that we are doing the reverse. This exclusion, now, is the cause of their heresy; and ignorance that we hold the other truth is the cause of their objections.

'First example: Jesus Christ is God and man. The Arians, unable to join these things which they think incompatible, say that he is man: in this they are Catholics. But they deny that he is God: in this they are heretics. They assert that we deny his humanity: in this, they are ignorant.'

Could it be said better in as few words as Pascal's?

But once we know how changing is the human heart, how hasty, how incapable of encompassing several things at once, how subject to passion and ready to take scandal; once we realize how the incarnation in the world of the Good Tidings compels the Church to take on the coloring of the world; when we understand also how greatly the political forces at work in history want to harness the religious drive to their own purpose, we are led to think that —except for an unlikely assistance which is not one of God's methods—divisions among Christians are *in fact* unavoidable. And if we admit, as Catholics do, that the axis of development founded on Peter and his successors will last forever, all probabilities to the contrary notwithstanding, we must expect to see all around this axis whole sheaves of separate and deviant developments, spiritual 'shoots' sprung from the tree trunk, and cut off from it to have their own separate history. And so the history of Christianity as a whole would not be unlike the evolution of species as Bergson saw it: a creative drive upon a privileged axis; and, drawing away from that axis, branches that do not follow its direction, that split and multiply or stop growing and stop sharing in the drive, but that are nonetheless always capable of reunification and, in a sense, are always ready to turn back towards the axis, to reunite in it: such is the hope of every ecumenical mind. Circumstances without precedent can bear it in upon the consciences of Christians, and the Divine will can make it happen.

St Augustine already linked the heresies to permanent types of thought. I have tried constantly to apply this typological method, in the thought that the number of possible positions which man's intellect can take up in regard to any problem (such as that of Jesus, or Joan of Arc . . .) is not very large, and that the various solutions recur under other names. The history of heresies offers me virgin territory in which to verify the mores of the mind. If the truth, in all areas and especially in the area of revealed religion, consists in a delicate structure made up of levels and perspectives that to us seem at variance with each other, then it is unavoidable, I said, that the intellect should try to isolate one aspect at the expense of all the others, and take it for the center of the whole. This, by the way, is how philosophy developed: every philosopher selects within the whole one point of view agreeable to him, denies what contradicts it, and sets about reconstructing the system of being around this single point which he calls *his* intuition, *his* philosophy. So that it could be said that philosophy renews itself by that very process which in religion, and especially in Christianity, produces doctrinal perspectives that are aberrations because they are exclusive—those arbitrary choices we call 'heresies'.

Heresy, like negation, does in fact have two aspects. The one, purely negative, stands out in strong relief—it is the only one that has been handed on in the dogmatic language of the anathemata of the Roman Church.

But there is a second aspect of heresy, less clearly visible, of no interest in daily practice, negligible from a pastoral viewpoint: and that is its positive, at times prophetic side. If we could take a long term view of history, we would notice that heresy has the marks of an exclusive emphasis, an excessive effort, an over-rash desire, a blooming in advance of season, a miscarriage of evolution. But *when the time will have come*—then this effort, this emphasis, this desire, this evolutionary urge may once more be introduced into the vital axis, recovered by the integral truth, reunited to the communion. Under this aspect one might say that several of the heretics are like bastard prototypes, imperfect and precocious—too precocious, of what some day will be accomplished. 'Montanus,' said Newman, 'is like a type of Francis of Assisi.'

If we were to pursue still further these views which try to justify that which is good within evil, we might say that the anguish of dismemberment, like every great pain, is the herald of fulness. The dismemberment, then, has two aspects. The first, negative and negating, is too obvious to tarry over. It is the sin against unity; and though the responsibilities of every individual are wrapped in mystery, objectively the fault lies with him who breaks away. This is what the Church cannot ever stop saying, since Christ has given unity into her charge, and since she has the vocation to suffer for that unity, and to be misunderstood because of the vocation.

But in every dismemberment (and any war is ultimately a war between the dis-united) there is also a positive aspect, an obscure promise. Every conflict may be a way of sorrows toward an equilibrium of a higher order. The highest and most lasting syntheses in this world never happen without pangs of pain. At the very heart of the battle of brother against brother, a trained eye could discern the outline of this synthesis already virtually present. Blood is what makes *of two*, *one*, said the Apostle. Christ is dismembered in the division of his faithful. Dismembered, he yet does not cease to be. And as being and unity are intimately connected, he cannot be unless he is at bottom still *one*. Dismembered, he yet cannot resign himself to it: he labors to restore his joints, his consistence, and his glory. Those who are in the center, in the travail of love and purification, are straining to prepare the reunion of the members. The disjointed members, in the travail of the desire for unity, and by virtue of the invisible circulation of oneness, tend on their part to join with one another, and then to join, together, the head crowned with thorns.

If I may propose a new expression, I would say that 'heresy'—it, too—has two aspects. One is the aspect of *secession* which so leaps to the eye. The other, visible to none but the patient observer who tries to sound out tendencies, interpret signs, hear the *unutterable groanings*, is the aspect which I would call *incession*. *Incession*, the movement complementary to the *secession* which seems at moments able to compensate for and abolish the secession —what is it? It is a movement toward return, an aspiration toward reunion of the members, reintegration, mystical and visible communion, Holy Supper possible once again together, RE-UNION in the fullest sense of this paradoxical word.

If there are deep inward values in what we call 'heresy', that are undeveloped or imprisoned, sibylline forebodings, a premature attempt at final synthesis; if, on the other hand, there is in the treasure-house of souls a store of mystic sufferings and yearnings, a constant and cleansing passion: then clearly Mother Church, who suffers the same sorrows, who knows the rich treasures that are kept outside her, should wish to become worthy of taking them to her once again. These are the days when the Pope did not hesitate to call upon the Church to make the effort to achieve a greater depth, a greater breadth, renewal, openness —so that the separated Churches might understand that by a reintegration they would lose nothing of the substantive and prophetic which they now possess; that, on the contrary, they would possess it more fully because their partial patrimony would rejoin the total patrimony which, in turn, would be purified of what at present defaces it.

In this spirit, and guided by these underlying views, I offer some *considerations* on some of the great crises of Christianity.

The world of living creatures brings us face to face with an immense variety of species. These species, however, may be grouped according to a few broad structural types, such as the vertebrates. In the same way, I have left to one side the varieties of doctrines, and dealt here only with a few leading ideas which I take to be perennially vital.

The first crisis to which I turned was the primal crisis, since I believe that one must study origins in order to find a prefiguration of what is to come.

The first crisis was that in which the Christians, emerged from paganism, separated themselves from the Jews to whom the gospel had been proclaimed. A formidable problem: in order to become Jesus's disciple, did one have to follow the example of Jesus,

the Apostles, the first believers, and practise the Jewish religion
or be associated with it? And, since Jesus had not clearly
settled this problem, how was one to interpret *the intent of the
Spirit?*

It was St Paul's solution which prevailed. One can be a
Christian without being a Jew. Soon the Christians that came
from Judaism were to be extinct. What would have happened
without St Paul's initiative? Such questions may at least be
raised. They are still alive: they remain on the horizon of the
Jewish question.

The gnostic crisis raised the problem of the relation between
faith and reason, which was to dominate all Western history.
Christianity, on the point of achieving self-awareness, found
itself face to face with the tradition and apparatus of Greek
thought. Would Christianity assimilate it? Or would it be
assimilated by Greek thought? That more expert knowledge of
the data of faith which is called *Gnosis*, the soil on which all
theology thrives, and which theology may adopt, correct, or
reject—in what form would it make its appearance? Gnosis, as
we have recently come to realize, is in fact prior to Greek
thought: it is a rather wide-spread type of thought, a category
of the intellect, an archetype. It offers a crude solution of the
problem of evil by the admission of two eternal principles, the
principle of Good and the principle of Evil, which divide between
them the dominion over being and over men. In this form,
obviously, gnosticism could not blend into Christianity, which
sees evil as a result of freedom. But the gnostic spirit is always
present, and in our own day continues to inspire philosophies and
politics.

With gnosticism, there also arises anew the constant problem
of knowing the relation between Christianity and Judaism: for
Marcion, the God of the Old Testament was a wicked God. Had
the Church followed Marcion—who did in fact shake her, because
he seemed to represent a continuation, though excessive, of St
Paul—she would have ended up in a sort of 'monochristianism';
a religion of the Christ in the pure state, without historical
context, without preparatory development.

Here, in the comparison of these two types of thought—that
of the Judeo-Christians, that of the gnostics—we can already see

the constant attitude of the Church in the face of dangers of contrasting type. She must maintain her links with the Jewish past, and yet again she must show here originality, her transcendence. She must assimilate what was best in her environment, and on the other hand, in order to avoid being herself assimilated, she must define her originality by relating herself to what is best in all the world. This oscillation between the two tendencies, toward the world (modernism) and toward inviolateness (integrism), always remains: it inheres in the very situation of the Church, forever in danger of yielding either to the *maximum* or to the *minimum* and, it might be said, an excess either of charity or else of love for her integrity.

The Arian crisis is no doubt the most remarkable from both the dogmatic and the political point of view. It could be called eminently *theologico-political*: it introduced an era in which theology and politics will always be more or less closely linked.

Toward the year 380, the Church barely missed turning semi-Arian overnight. The mystery of the incarnation was being put in question, and was reduced to a solution more in conformity with specious reason: Christ was merely this superman, this saint, this 'chief of mystics' who might be taken for the dim goal of Evolution. Henceforth, the Christian mystery was 'de-mystified' or, in Bultmann's term, 'de-mythologized'. And now that the Word had been emptied, and theology had become like philosophy, the gospel was acceptable to the well-informed, the moderate, the cultivated; the politic, conciliatory, imperial mind; the mystic, romantic, poetic mind. To a Roman no less than to a barbarian, everything was now clearer and more attractive in this religion which had demoted the Christ-God, and thereby made it possible to save the failing Empire and even to take into it the young barbarian nations. Arianism, in my view, is the archetype of Illusion. It is the Christian 'heresy' closest to orthodoxy—by all appearances; the most human and most civilizing—by all appearances; the most inviting to the splendors of the world, of the intellect, of generosity—by all appearances. The most 'catholic' by all appearances, in its reliance on Jewish and Christian Scriptures and its respect for the earliest ecclesiastical tradition. And also the most adroit, by its subtleties, its metamorphoses, its middle-of-the-road, conciliating, and ambiguous forms.

I turn next to Islam. Islam is not, of course, a heresy within Christianity, but a crisis analogous to the crisis of heresies, and perhaps the most obdurate by the sheer length of its effect. One could approximate Islam to Judaism, and see in it a Judaism simplified and accommodated to the oriental mentality; just as Arianism was a Christianity simplified for the Egyptians, the Romans and the Germans. But in contrast to heresy, it was from the start an enemy from outside which proceeded by material conquest; it nearly destroyed Christianity by occupying the earth; after twelve centuries it remains impenetrable to Christianity, threatens it still, stops it short at every turn—and does so in spite of the common belief in One God. What a mystery it is, of times past and still more of the present!

Next, I shall study the Catharist crisis in the Middle Ages, which is the first form of a revolt against the cultural and social aspects of medieval Christianity, of the return to a certain gospel, a first attempt to recover radical 'purity': the separation from the world carried to the extreme which is the condemnation of the flesh in its function to transmit life. The Catharist spirit has not ceased being active in the West. The problems raised by the relations, always so difficult to fix, between spirit and flesh, between the ideal and the real, between the exigencies of perfection and adjustment, between counsel and precept—they are as much alive today as in the days of the Catharists. Our modern literature, politics, mystiques, our conception of love and of sex are shot through with Catharist trends. The modern intellect and modern passion are still tainted with Catharism and dolorism.

Finally I shall deal with the Reformation. I have tried to understand this schism which is so vast, so deep, so nearly unforeseeable, seemingly all but irreparable, and which has had so great an influence upon the destiny of the West. The theologico-political phenomenon that is the mark of serious separation is here in full view. The fundamental problem as I see it is this: to understand in what sense the Reformation is a heresy in Christianity, and whether it is not rather a much more radically different idea which could have made its appearance either much sooner, or else much later, or even at the present time, for which the crisis of the 16th century was only the occasion. What is this essence of the Reformation, translated into the terms of current thought? That is what I have tried to define and to express, with the intent to uncover the scar more fully, but by that token also to render the matter less insoluble. For this is the issue on which, at the heart of the world of the Reformation, and at the heart of the world of Catholicism, there rises up the ecumenical hope.

The last chapter belongs in the half-light of this hope and this danger, while the Council is in suspense. About the present moment it remains silent. I plan to complete it when the time is ripe, in a study that will define the relation of Vatican II with the crisis of the present time and the development of the Gospel.

This is a short book, made up of omissions, marked by breaks and ellipses, like a poem. An evening book—I mean of the evening of life; I hope we are not at the evening of history. There is no time: I must make my will.

It seems to me that a thought structure which is independent, but which like mine has been born, raised, and reached its growth in the Catholic Church, implies an effort to achieve a universal view of history. I have said elsewhere[1] that I see Catholicism as the form of the All, the axis of evolution, and more: the *locus* of the final recapitulation. This is to say that every partial view of history is unfavourable to Catholicism and, conversely—as St Paul and St Augustine sensed—that every complete, comprehensive, dynamic view is favorable to it.

The fault in a book like this one is that it is tied to the substance of its author. It is marked by my ideas, my failings, my regrets, and also by my hopes. I am sure to be told that I lack objectivity, that I have shown myself too sincere, too naked. And yet, I keep thinking that the more one puts *one's own* thought into a study as wide-ranging as this, inviting the reader to do the same, the more one works for the development of historical studies. The higher education of the Germans, the Anglo-Saxons, the Italians favors essays of this kind more than does ours. Why?

[1] In *Vers L'Unité Dans L'Amour*.

I do not know. Daniel Halévy, Denis de Rougemont, Robert Aron (who gave me the stimulus for this book) have opened the road for me. There are times when a man must venture forth all by himself, like a simple soldier who takes over when the chiefs are dead.

Definition and Dates

'All authority in heaven and on earth has been given to me. Go therefore and make disciples of all nations, baptizing them in the name of the Father and of the Son and of the Holy Spirit, teaching them to observe all that I have commanded you; and lo, I am with you always, to the close of the age.'
St Matthew 28, 18-20

'As the Father knows me and I know the Father; and I lay down my life for the sheep.

'And I have other sheep, that are not of this fold; I must bring them also, and they will heed my voice. So there shall be one flock, one shepherd.'
St John 10, 15-16

IN THIS WORK I DEAL WITH THE CHURCH AS THE HISTORIC form taken among men by the permanence of Jesus Christ in time. The Catholic Church thus is the Christ continued. But she has children among those who are strangers to her, just as she has enemies among her children: the *soul* of the Church does not coincide with her body, that is, with the visible aspect of the Catholic Church. This is traditional doctrine.

The Church is like a *dismembered Christ* because of the division among Christians. Yet this dismemberment, which is an agony, does not rob her of her unity, her life, her fulness. For the Catholic Church is the unique structure of salvation around which, at the time decreed by God, the visible unity of Christians and men of good will must reconstitute itself.

This Catholic viewpoint has inspired my manner of expression, and has prompted me to adopt certain terms that have been current in Europe for centuries.

I call *schism* (after a Greek word meaning *division*) a separation from the Catholic Church which carries with it only a minimal divergence in doctrine. I call *heresy* (after a Greek word meaning *choice*) a separation that is due to a doctrinal divergence. The word 'orthodoxy' (after a Greek word meaning 'right opinion')

27

designates the Eastern Churches separated from Rome since the eleventh century and especially the Russian Church. In this book we do not deal with schisms, since we are interested in doctrinal crises.

Schism and heresy are known since the beginnings of Christianity. Considering the conditions under which the Church developed, their appearance could have been foreseen. In order to live on through space and time, the Christian leaven had to be mixed with the human dough. It was almost inevitable that in the process it should be adulterated.

At the birth of Christianity the danger was twofold: it threatened from Judaism, and it threatened from paganism.

Judeo-Christians, 'Judaisers', and at times, Ebionites, is the name given to those Christians who seceded toward the end of the first century because they held the Jewish observances to be necessary for salvation, and because they had come to see in Jesus an ordinary man.

Gnostics is the name given to those Christians of the second century who mixed elements of pagan philosophy into the doctrine of the Apostles. *Gnostic* derives from *gnosis*, a Greek term meaning knowledge; the gnostics set the enlightened and knowing faith of the informed Christian against the rude faith of the Christians. To solve the problem of evil, gnosticism claimed the existence of two eternal principles, the principle of Good and the principle of Evil. This doctrine, which took many faces, developed in the second century, and became the inspiration of eminent men among whom Basilides, Valentinus, and Marcion are the best-known. The doctrine of Montanus (about 156 AD), called 'Montanism', is a form of gnosticism based on absolute purism and on the expectation of a new revelation of the Holy Spirit. One of the most powerful minds of the times, Tertullian of Carthage, became a Montanist.

Arianism is the heresy of Arius. Though Arius continued to call the Word by the name of God in order to conform with current usage, he maintained that Jesus is not God but merely the most perfect of created beings. Arius was condemned at the Council of Nicaea (325), the first ecumenical council, where the Catholic faith was defined by that formula which is sung in the

Definition and Dates

Roman Mass: 'I believe in Jesus Christ, the Son of God, God of God, Light of Light, consubstantial with the Father.'

After the Nicene Council, Arian tendencies gathered fresh force, and took the form of rather subtle doctrines among which the best-known is Semi-Arianism. This was condemned in 381, at the second ecumenical council of Constantinople, at which the formulation of Nicaea was completed with these words concerning the Holy Spirit: 'The Lord and Giver of Life, who proceeds from the Father and the Son; who together with the Father and Son is adored and glorified; who spoke through the prophets.'

While the Church spread in the West, she was snuffed out in the East and in Africa by Mohammed (570-632) who broke with both Jews and Christians (622). His religion was called 'Islam', because it demanded complete surrender to the One God.

The Catharists, so called after a Greek word meaning 'pure', were originally ascetics who by self-abnegation meant to protest against the decadence of Christian morals. Their doctrine spread in Southern France and Northern Italy around the eleventh and twelfth centuries. They were crushed in a war of twenty years (1209-29) known as 'the Albigensian Crusade'.

The Reformation, or Protestantism, is the name given to the attempt of the German monk Luther and the Frenchman Jean Calvin to reform the abuses from which the Church had been suffering for two centuries, and to protest against a number of doctrines and Church traditions. In consequence of the political situation of the time, the actions of these two initiators had very far-reaching effects. The Catholic Church met in Council at Trent (1542-63) to put an end to controversy and re-establish unity. However, the Protestants did not recognize the Council. The Council of Trent began the reform of the Church that has become known as the 'Counter-Reformation'. It gave vigorous expression to the Catholic doctrine of grace and the sacraments. The Catholic Church recovered a consciousness of her vitality and her unity. It faced up to the future.

To pave the way for the union of Christians, to bring the Church up to date, and to allow her to brave the new age in a world threatened by atomic destruction, and smitten with equality and unity, Pope John XXIII called an ecumenical council which met at the Vatican on October 11, 1962. Its first session lasted until December 8, 1962. Pope John was to die on June 3, 1963. He was replaced by Pope Paul VI, who intends to continue the work of the council in the same spirit.

The word 'ecumenical' (which means 'of all the inhabited earth') has in these days two distinct meanings which are, however, often confused.

Used as an adjective together with the word 'Council', it means a council which is not local, provincial, or national, but which brings together all the bishops attached to Rome, under the presidency of the Pope or a Papal delegate. It is generally agreed that there have been twenty-one councils prior to 1962. The ecumenical councils after the Eastern schism are not recognized by the Orthodox Churches, nor by the Churches that stem from the Reformation.

The words *ecumenical, ecumenism* have taken on a new meaning in the last twenty years. They now denote the movements of conciliation, of an attempt at union and unity, that have sprung up among Protestants and among Catholics. Protestant ecumenism tends to re-unite the diverse Protestant confessions in a single profession of faith; as its highest goal, it aims for a visible union of all Christians.

Catholic ecumenism is alert to the religious, Christian, even Catholic values that are present in the separated Churches. It intends to prepare for that moment when a renewed Catholic Church will re-unite within herself all Christians in a single visible body, in fulfilment of the prayer of the Lord Jesus before the sacrifice of the Cross.

'I do not pray for these only, but also for those who believe in me through their word, that they may all be one; even as thou, Father, art in me, and I in thee, that they also may be in us, so that the world may believe that thou hast sent me. . . . I made known to them thy name, and I will make it known, that the love with which thou hast loved me may be in them, and I in them. St John 17, 20-6*

Judaism

THERE OFTEN IS A GAP IN HUMAN AFFAIRS BETWEEN
what we expect and what does happen. The very term *event*
denotes surprise. That gap was no doubt never more striking
than when Christianity came into being. Jesus stands out against
the background of a rising expectation: the expectation of the
Messiah. But even while he fulfills the prophecy he gives it the
lie, contradicts and sublimates it.

Jesus did not mean to found a new religion. In his historical
humanity, Jesus was a devout Israelite, practising the law to the
full, from circumcision to Pasch, paying the half-shekel for the
Temple. Jerusalem, capital of his nation, was the city he loved:
Jesus wept over it. Jesus had spiritually realized the germinal
aspiration of his people, which was to raise the God of Israel
high enough to make of him, forever, the God of all peoples.
What Jesus did proclaim had been proclaimed before. In a sense,
except for his accent of absolute authority, nearly everything he
said had been said before or at the very least had been dimly
revealed and promised.

His first disciples, even while they believed that Jesus was
the Messiah and more than the Messiah, remained like their
master devout and faithful Jews. They had no thought of cutting
back in any manner the practices of the law. What they added—
baptism in the name of Jesus, the breaking of the Bread in the
homes, the teaching of the New Tidings—all this, it seems, could
very well be adopted, and then adapted to the religion of Noah,
of Abraham, or of Moses and the prophets; somewhat like the
rites and methods and the spirit of a new religious order (of
Francis of Assisi, for example, or of the Little Brothers of Father
Charles de Foucauld) take their place in the Catholic edifice
that began with Jesus, as a new branch sprouts on an old oak
tree.

Yet a keen observer would have seen that the situation was
unstable, that in this form it could not last.

Let fifty years go by, and see what has happened. Certain
Jews have rejected, condemned, and stoned Jesus's disciples.

Several pagans, on the other hand, have become converts without passing through the intermediary stage of Judaism: they have adhered directly to Jesus, who has found himself at the head of a new people. This was the accident, in a way essential, that marked out this origination.

If that accident could occur so soon after the beginning, the reason is no doubt that it was not quite so accidental. Yet it is strange that it came about so rapidly. But if the unforeseeable genius Paul had not appeared, if the unforeseeable fall of Jerusalem had not taken place—it is certain that some day, in consequence of reflection or of this or that inevitable circumstance, it would have become patent that the religion of Jesus was, in fact, a new religion, and that it had found in the religion of Israel no more than a preparation, henceforth finished. The Sanhedrin had divined as much within the hour, with the lucidity of hate.

From the viewpoint of the first believers, and no doubt even of the opponents, the shocking surprise was that the coming of Jesus the Messiah did not stop short the course of history. Strangely, unthinkably, time went on. The end of the world was deferred. There was a reprieve! And Jesus had foreseen an establishment within this time of reprieve. He had taken steps to found a society of the faithful, capable of extending through space by preaching, through time by succession. Jesus had truly founded a new order.

And now that history did not end, now that it even seemed to begin spiritually—since in Jesus the God of Abraham could be proclaimed to the entire then inhabited world—it became necessary to distinguish, within the whole heritage of Israel which Jesus and his Apostles had accepted, that which was obsolete and accidental from what was lasting and essential.

This separation of accident and essence is always and in every way the task that is for each man, and for all men, supreme and difficult. Where to lay the axe? How to conceive that division?

It is noteworthy that Jesus gave no guidance in this matter which to us seems basic. If we are to speak of Jesus as a man, who did not know the future, we must say that he did not consider the normal entrance of the pagans into his own sphere as anything more than their admission to the fellowship of Israel. True, he found faith in the Roman centurion. And he saved the pagans, in the moment of their conversion, without Israel. But if the centurion wanted to go on living the life of God, he could do so only by taking part in the Jewish cult: at any rate Jesus does not indicate that the centurion could gain salvation in any other way than by belonging to Israel.

At this point a stock-taking became necessary, and that stock-taking called for a local meeting, practically a spatial communion of leaders in prayer. This was, in fact, a council, the first council. There was assembly, colloquium, discussion, the labor of collective thought in order to arrive at a unanimous decision on what would have to be demanded of the converts as necessary to give them the right to the new grace of Jesus Christ.

It will be useful to reflect on the differences between what could have happened and what, in fact, did happen, in order to throw light upon the improbable: namely, the historical event, with all the force and meaning of the word *evenit*: 'it happened that . . .' which always carries a measure of amazement before what is.

A priori, in all questions of this kind placed before a community or a council, opinions divide into three areas: those of the two extremes, that of the middle.

In this instance:

> One might impose Judaism on everyone.
> One might impose Judaism on no-one.
> One might chart a middle course.

And here again, there were two possible emphases, as the middle solution tended toward one extreme or toward the other.

We learn from history that conflicts did arise within the earliest communities between the 'Hebrews' and the 'Hellenists'. *The Acts of the Apostles* report the scruples of Peter when he was informed by the Holy Spirit that he would have to baptize in Caesarea the Roman centurion Cornelius: a pagan! Peter raised the basic objection; he saw that the Gospel had been given not only to the Jews but to all nations. But what demands was he to make of this newly-Christian pagan?

To understand the difficulty, let us imagine that Catholicism might gain followers among a de-Christianized proletariat—but that these adepts though sincerely Catholic or eager to become

35

Catholic, hesitate to join in all of Christian practice, which seems to them overburdened with adventitious elements: for example, they do not accept the cult of saints, or weekly mass. Understandably, then, those responsible in the Church ask themselves just what will have to be required. They will consider the possibility of a preparatory liturgy, a catechumenate, perhaps a simplification of duties. Every society that has undergone a long development which caused it to mature, but also to increase though it remained unchanged, is forced into such purifying self-examination—especially so when it is faced with beings who are new and without history, or without the same history, who yet want to share its life, and who bring with them the drive, the freshness, the apostolic fervor within them. No doubt Europe's situation will be such with regard to the black or yellow peoples that would join her.

All these are but clumsy analogies. For in the case of early Christianity, the distinction between *essence* and *accident* cut to the heart of the matter. It involved all prior and all future history.

An event intervened that could not have been foreseen in any way whatever: the arrival, out of a clear sky, of a religious genius, perhaps the greatest religious genius in all the history of Christendom; at least if by *genius* we mean this rarest gift that is like a concentrate of the power to foresee with the power to see, the prophetic power with the philosophic power, and by virtue of which the essence of any problem stands out in an absolute, calm, transfigured light above whatever is not of the essence. This power, like any complete power, may be prone to illusion—and so drag a leader and his followers into wayward adventures charged with consequence. But if it points toward truth and toward the future, what an advantage!

Paul saw clearly that with Christ everything had become new, transformed forever, sublimated—and that this renewal, a completion not an abolition, called for an absolute, radical reinterpretation to the very core of everything that till now had been taught, thought, prescribed in the declarations, the rites, the methods, the diffusion, the hopes, the joys, the possessions—in everything, absolutely everything. And Paul comprehended that the Jewish Law could save no longer, but only the Faith in Jesus Christ.

It seems that the deacon Stephen had almost seen this. But there is an infinity between an *almost* and an *all*. Christ's return, in the eyes of the martyr deacon whose sight was already fixed on God, was not to abrogate the Law but to restore it in its original purity. He blamed the degenerate cult of the Temple, not the Law of Moses.

As for the Fathers of the first council, they did not follow Paul absolutely. Mutual concessions are exchanged. The viewpoint of St Peter remains quite different from that of St Paul. Paul's liberalism with regard to the Mosaic law is tolerated for missionary reasons: in order not to rebuff from the outset the pagan peoples to whom the Apostle was addressing himself, they will be spared the Jewish stage. But the same concession cannot be made to the Jewish Christians who remained in Palestine. They still live in the shadow of the Temple, cling to the past. In an effort at conciliation, St Paul requires the circumcision of his disciple Timothy, born of a Jewish mother and a Greek father. St Paul himself consents to pass through a 'Nazirite' retreat, so as not to give rise to the calumnies of fanatics. But this same St Paul, distinguishing the spirit from the letter, is to find the definitive word; 'There is no longer either Jew or pagan, either circumcised or uncircumcised . . .'

The Council of Jerusalem, as often happens in such cases, chose a middle way. One could decree that pagans who desired to follow Jesus would be subjected to none of the Jewish observances: that was St Paul's thought. Or else, that they had to become Jews. The Council subjected them to a *minimum*.

Paul kept quiet. He thought himself satisfied. This decision, under the appearance of conciliation, involved in fact the whole future, because it made salvation independent of the practice of the Jewish law. But Paul saw further: as I have said, he had understood (doubtless within an instant, because these total conversions can happen only *in instanti*, in a flash) that among the elements vital to the Israelite community, certain ones would have to be rejected forever. Such were the theocracy, the cult in a temple, the sacrifice of animals, the tie to a country, to a race. Others could be preserved: such were the Scripture scrolls. Still others, finally, would have to be sublimated, that is, carried over into a transcendent order where they would live on in a nobler way: such as the decalogue, the teaching about God, the circumcision, the Pasch, the priesthood, justice, ardor. And Paul, with his Israelite and transfiguring genius, saw and understood that this sublimation did not mean that the new Israel would be in the domain of the intellect, invisible, above attack, eternal even now, abstracted from the institution, detached from earth, but that on the contrary this Israel called Church would have to rearrange the organisation of its dealings with the world, find for them a new, simpler style, more human and more universal, with a new hierarchy replacing the twelve tribes: the group of the Twelve, with a new authority in place of the authority of Moses or the High Priest: the authority of Peter-Cephas. And this because Jesus is the true Son of God. From now on it is He who is the race, the country, the patrimony: the divine heritage is henceforth and forever at our disposal, through THE SON.

The Israelite community could doubtless have achieved this transformation and, by self-sublimation, become a divine community.

In fact, among all the peoples of antiquity, and perhaps of all times, the Jewish people was the best suited to comprehend a radical historical change. Everything prepared the Jews for it— their ideas, customs, hopes, their faith straining toward a radical change of the times. The idea that one person could herald, signify another, as Abraham prefigured Moses, the idea of a forever possible new beginning, the idea of recapitulation within the seed—all this the Jews possessed and even had *lived* already more than once. And in a sense, Paul was a Jew of genius who completed certain thoughts of his people, by applying them to *thinking* Jesus Christ.

Paul desired with all his heart that his people share his intuition and his course of action. Israel, then, by lowering a little the barrier of all those observances, would in Jesus have accepted the Christ, and in the Christ, God. And there would have been a Judeo-Christian Church, which the best of the pagans would have joined as 'proselytes' of the second order.

But Paul saw that the history of Israel decreed otherwise. In the eyes of the Apostle, Israel refused that solution. Israel, as represented by its Jerusalemite leaders, refused to die and open itself. Jerusalem preferred to kill and close itself. Her Law protected her against paganism, but Israel did not agree to lift this Law up to the Faith in Jesus so that it might escape literal Judaism and find again true Judaism.

Thus, Israel has stopped short in its development. It has remained like a plant without bloom, a root without issue, a witness only. So thinks St Paul and, after him, so think most Christians. Paul saw more clearly than anyone else, and saw at once, that the refusal which Israel addressed to the Christian sublimation would bring in its train a change in God's plan for the salvation of mankind, as Adam's fall had done once in the beginning. Within the former plan, Israel could have passed, without a jolt, by peaceable conversion, from the particular to the universal.

But the first plan of growth was not to happen. That plan of development and of continuity was displaced by a plan of excrescence and dismemberment, struggle and 'dialectic' in Hegel's sense, in which the fulness of being would be achieved not by slow assimilation, by the progressive passing from one to the other, but by antithesis, war and violent rupture, death and separation, the interim triumph of mediocrity, the persecution of the pure, the reduction of the pure to a small, persecuted remnant that is miraculously kept and saved each time.

What Paul also saw, and said, was that this drastic change of plan, this passage from 'development' to 'dialectic', had an enormous practical advantage: it would allow a sudden extension of Israel, a substitution of the law of space, which is almost instantaneous multiplication, for the law of time, which is axial and gradual growth. In short a vast cast of the net could now be attempted, because the non-Jews were in a more favourable position than the Jews to accept from the start, in a form detached from prior history and hence profoundly simplified, THE ESSENCE, WHICH MEANS CHRIST, THE CHRIST ALONE.

That Paul's insight was deep, from a point of view at once theoretical, practical, and mystical—of this there is no doubt. If genius can be defined by the simplicity and speed of its insight, on the level of thought and on the level of action, Paul was a genius. And he is of the highest order, he who was historically the most successful, the second inventor of the Christianity which was contained in the work of Jesus but which the Jesus of history had not expressed so plainly.

Did not Paul perhaps precipitate the rupture?

Could it be that Peter's patience, though less aware, was perhaps more profound? In plain fact, Paul did succeed in *founding* Christianity to the ends of the known world; and while he was not the first to come to Rome, he died at Rome with Peter. The Church of Rome has conciliated them. For the rest, Paul saw full well that Israel was not *rejected* but only momentarily cut off. The people of his origin was to him a people that is witness, still waiting, for whom there was reserved a final task because its divine gifts could never be lost.

Therefore, the first crisis of Christianity, and the imprint it left on the original substance of Christianity is beyond doubt the most important one Christianity has known. It was short, decisive, headlong—under the pressure of necessity, and by the action of one person. The pressure of events, of the exigencies of the missions, and above all the pressure of success, are all on one side of the scale.

I strike Paul out of history. I ask myself, as we may and should do with so many outstanding men, what would have happened if he had not lived. What would have happened if the Church had not broken with Judaism so early and so radically, if the Christians had remained Judeo-Christians, if sacrifice had been continued in Jerusalem, if the Law had been fulfilled, not being properly annulled? Most certainly the Greek world would not have been conquered so quickly; would it not have been conquered in the long run, in spite of everything? The dynamism of the Jewish race coupled with the proselytism of the new Christians gathered to Israel, would it not have sustained the Church? Since the Jewish problem would not have arisen, the powers of the chosen race would have been at the service of the new religion. Those powers might have preserved Christianity from certain deviations which have given rise to heresies. Could Mohammedanism have arisen in such a Judeo-Christian world?

What would have happened in the long run if the pagans had rebelled against the teaching of Jesus, if they had thought it too Jewish, too oriental, or too exacting? If Jesus had converted a large number of Jews? In short, what would have happened if the first plan of Jesus and the Apostles had had the sanction of a huge success? In that case the way of James 'brother of the Lord' would have prevailed. And Paul would have been left in a secondary, almost abnormal position. Paulinism might have produced a 'heresy' split off from the trunk, a kind of *archeo-protestantism*. Christ would indeed have been dismembered! At a minimum, the Judeo-Christian religion would have been marked with an original stain, that of comprising two types of faithful of which one would be privileged above the other. There would have been two kinds of believers: those by tradition, race, and with every right, and those who were believers by adoption and, as it were, by conquest. However, juxtapositions without symbiosis do not last, especially in this two-headed Church in which the convert-wing would have been the one to move forward.

But this supposition did not become a reality, and Jesus's religion was quickly obliged to separate itself from the Jewish religion. What is more, we soon see the Jewish religion opposing that of Jesus, at times with exceeding harshness. These conflicts, by compelling Jesus's party to set itself apart and to be the whole Church, gave it two advantages that as a rule are mutually exclusive: that of being extremely ancient, and that of being extremely new. The religion *was born*, since it took life from Jesus, with the supple, tender organs of the newly-born, as inarticulate and as powerful as a seed. Though born without wrinkles, it was already ancient, having behind it all of the Jewish tradition. The Old Testament was the Law of its prayer and its cult. The Church was the fulfilment of the 'Law and the Prophets'. Time was fulfilled. Jesus Christ had been the issue of all that preceded him. A race, more than one institution, a people, a past—all this was summed up in one person.

Concerning time, we might say (as Leon Brunschvicg once remarked to me) that at that moment we are face to face with the very problem of Time itself: the most impressive realization of the *before* and the *after*, both the experience and the striking illustration of that mysterious and constant phenomenon we call CHANGE—I mean, the sudden and decisive change which the illusion of evolution often hides from us.

That problem of abrupt change has not faced the Jews only. It is known to all peoples in their crises and revolutions. It arises for every society that shows growth in its ways of understanding and of action, and that yet wishes to remain faithful to that within itself which is its special gift, essence, and heritage. This need, incidentally, to maintain continuity with their most ancient state is much less strong in modern peoples: because of the triumph of Christianity, a people holds its past no longer sacred.

The consequence of Christianity's surge was to render the Jewish situation paradoxical. Christianity had surged forth (as did the human species, according to some anthropologists) from a premature birth. There are those who say that the first man was a simian embryo, incompletely developed and born too soon: an initial miscarriage, biologically speaking, summoned the Spirit down upon its animal nature. So here: this rupture, due to Paul who speaks of himself as a premature convert, *ektroma*, an 'abortion', allowed Christian freedom to show itself totally and from the very start, without a slow unfolding. For the religion of Moses it was a rending trial, surely undeserved: the enemies of Jesus 'did not know what they were doing'. But the Christian leaven, out of its wrappings, appeared in all its purity.

At this point Israel might raise a friendly objection: 'It cannot be denied, of course, that the separation of the Christians did have great advantages for the religion of Jesus. Christianity was free to assert its essence. But at what price! It found itself more malleable, more receptive to influences, more easily assimilated, and itself more ready to assimilate what could be taken over from the Greeks and Romans—the pagans. However, this temporal aspect, this naturalistic, Roman, and Hellenistic aspect which Christianity has taken on has made it far too worldly.

'Besides, the separation hastened the decline of the mother branch. It was the deathblow to the religion of Moses, of Abraham, of Noah, the religion which by a return to its sources, could become a larger, moral, universal monotheism—without strict obligations, without sacraments, without divisive rites, without unverifiable beliefs. Then a spiritual Israel could have appeared, safeguarding the traditions of the prophets, recovering the pre-Mosaic spirit. Israel would have been a dynamic religion at the heart of mankind, espousing history, to bring about awakenings, revolutions in the name of true justice.

'The development peculiar to the religion of Jesus is otherwise. It issues in mysteries, expressed in dogmas, that are quite different from the large mysteries of biblical Judaism which is a religion of faith, of hope, but not of dogmas. If Jesus had not been the Christ, we might have witnessed, as André Siegfried once said, the rise of a liberal and spiritualist Judaism, simpler in form and more acceptable to the mind of antiquity. It might have conquered Greece, Rome, the world—especially since everywhere a wind was blowing, much like the breath of the Jewish faith, which was drawing the élite to the God of the prophets, so far above the dwellers on Olympus, toward a religion of the spirit. Then the course of human history would have been different: one would have witnessed the rise of a sort of Arianism, nursing an unyielding, monotheistic sensitivity. The Christianity of St Paul would not have come to be, only the Gospel; and perhaps Islam might never have arisen? The Western separation of reason and faith, technique and mystique, critique and mystery would not have come about. Nothing would have been profane, everything would have been linked to God within a kind of time forever sacred, a perpetual Pasch.'

But to put the problem this way is only to bring out once more what separates: to wit, the belief in Christ as God, as the revealer of a divine mystery, whom Israel still will not recognize.

In our day, after such tremendous trials of the Jewish people, we see the deep mystical tradition of Israel finding expression in a new form: that of the Hassidim, the 'pious' always present in Israel, for whom humility and renunciation are the supreme values. In its élites, Israel has preserved its hunger for the God who is One and transcendent, and the universal love that follows. Robert Aron in his recent book, *Jesus of Nazareth: the Hidden Years*, shows that Jewish mysticism is in its essence far from dividing the universe into sacred and profane, as did the pagan and so many moderns after them. Jewish mysticism, instead, links every being, every event to God, without miracle and almost without mystery, in such a way that to a Jew all things are sacred, all things sacrament. If the Jewish mystics do not accept the Incarnation, they yet practise forms of union with God that do not, after all, exclude the hypothesis of a God carrying his friendship to the point of loving folly in the humiliation of the Incarnation. It could perhaps even be held that this sacral and intimate idea of persons and things reaches full bloom and sublimation in the idea of the *Word-become-flesh*. Whatever be the merit of this hope, which a Christian cannot keep from expressing, let us recognize with Robert Aron that the Jewish religion remains a religion in the strict sense, destined to perpetual effort, refusing all easy solutions, 'dodging no doubt and no suffering that lead to God'. The only question that from now on remains between Jews and Christians, purged of the resentments of their fathers and better informed of each other's beliefs and of their common roots, is this: to know, yes or no, whether the beloved of Israel, the Christ Jesus, Son of God, has not led us into the infinity of God; whether he is not of another order than all the other prophets; whether this fact, this mystery do not compel us to reverse our views of history, since Jesus, instead of being a point in that history, would be the fixed axis around which history turns.

That separation, so painful, of Jew and Christian, which St Paul was the first to seize dialectically, prolongs and realizes the mystery which the Gospel of John expresses in the gentlest and simplest way: 'And his own,' he says, 'received him not.'

In 62, the very year when St Paul had to defend his faith in Rome before Cæsar, his opponents, the Judaising Christians, were themselves being persecuted in Jerusalem. James, 'brother of the Lord', venerated by Jews and Christians alike for the austerity of his life and his long prayers in the Temple—he even was called *Obliam*, the Rampart of the People—was stoned at the command of Hanan II, the son of that same Anna whom we know from the recital of the Passion.

Four years later, an uprising of the anti-Roman underground in Judea was suppressed by terror. The Judaising Christians removed to Pella, a Hellenic town of the Decapolis. Jerusalem was razed, and turned into a Roman camp. Hadrian built a new city on the site, with a temple in the place of the Temple. There followed the revolt of Simon Bar-Kochba, who called himself the true Jesus, the long-awaited Messiah—and a fanatic war, a war of extermination for three years (132-5), that meant the material extinction of Judaism. It was then that the Jewish land took on the desert look which it has retained until the recent restoration of Israel.

The Jewish Christians were caught in a vice of conscience. Indifferent like Jesus to political régimes, they were pro-Roman rather than in revolt. The insurgents fell with fury upon their reasonable brothers who in their eyes were enemies worse than the Romans. But owing to the Roman victory, the Jewish Christians continued a timid existence. A colony, Aelia Capitolina, rose on the spot where once stood the Holy City. Jupiter sat enthroned above the site of the Temple. Golgotha sheltered a temple of Venus, divine protectress of Rome. Jews were forbidden on pain of death to stay in the city.

From that time on, a chasm separated the Jews from those Christians who had seemed collaborators. The Christians in turn thought the Jews much harder to convert than the pagans. Hatred arose between the two peoples, one unfaithful, the other faithful. From that time on, the Judaising Christians were set apart within the Church: their numbers dwindled, they grew sparse in the towns, and were cut off from one another, without hierarchy, dogmatics, or episcopate. They were not excommunicated, of course. Rather they received the kind of veneration that a young community in full vigor accords to the ancients who have been left behind forever, who have withdrawn into themselves, encapsuled in their faith.

As often happens within groups that are shut off too tightly, these purest of the pure produced schisms among themselves; they could not fight the changes of the faith. Integralist though they were in the practice of the Jewish law, they did, in a kind of compensation, allow to innovators freedom of thought and action. St Irenaeus and Origen treat the Judeo-Christians as no more than an inoffensive sect. They were called, without malice, Ebionim—the Poor. Obviously, they rejected the epistles of St Paul; the only gospel they accepted was that of St Matthew.

Still, as sometimes happens to emigrants on the move, they spread out—as far as Alexandria and Arabia. This fact was of vast consequence, since it is they from whom Mohammed learned in part what he knew of Christianity.

In the last thirty years, we have learned much about Judeo-Christian thought (the work of Father Dani lou is an example) which until then had been lost to history—as often happens to the vanquished.

Christianity developed on Greek soil. Its first Jewish shoots did not reach the daylight. Jewish theology of the time of Jesus was of an apocalyptic and visionary kind which saw in revelation the disclosure of all kinds of secrets; theological secrets of course, but also scientific and historical secrets. When this theology, remaining orthodox no matter what, came to deal with the gospel it would admit none but the Christ alone behind the Veil. It made him carry the full weight of this *gnosis*. Modern sensibility is more receptive to these Judeo-Christian attempts than was that of the past century. For we are living in less dissimilar times, times when the menace of a sudden end of time produces a feeling of precariousness. Men take an interest only in what can be completed, and think of it as if it were wholly contained in its completion. Only when evening falls, said Hegel, the owl—the thinking bird—takes wing. Besides, tired of knowledge and compartimentalization, we are more eager today than we were fifty years ago to see rising a structure of synthesizing thought that would make us understand the link of the divine events of the Incarnation with the evolutionary history of the worlds. The two extremes, *Alpha* and *Omega*, brought together by the vertiginous speed of historical time, touch *us*. The action of the *Word* is at the same time both cosmic and historic. These are the reasons which, together with the rapprochement of Christians and Jews under the impact of race persecutions, lend to that Judeo-Christianity a shimmer which Harnack in his *History of Dogma* did not mention.

The encounter between Christianity and Hellenism, which has continued down to our day—with intervals of oblivion but also with 'renaissances' of which Thomism is no doubt the most famous—has caused Judeo-Christian theology to remain under a cloud. That theology was to inspire above all the cult, the liturgy where we meet it at several points. But it was not to take hold in the Western mind.

Ought we to regret this fact? Or should we not rather welcome the chances of Providence which have decreed that theology shall deal only with the *sacred*, and not be held to reveal the profane; that it shall not do duty for scientific, historical, or philosophical research; in short, that theology is not *gnostic* but *agnostic*? It could be maintained that all Christian thought rises upon the ruins of a *gnosis*—if we must so define the confusion between the realm of faith and the realm of science.

Gnosticism

THE WORD 'GNOSTICISM' CALLS FOR A DEFINITION. I shall define it in two ways—first by the rôle it played in history, and then according to what it came to mean, in the logic of history.

Historically, *gnosticism* is the name commonly given to the first 'great heresy' which the Catholic Church encountered in the second century, when the period of the Apostles and their immediate successors had ended. The characteristic mark of that 'great heresy' was that it mixed Christianity with various thought structures that properly belonged to the Hellenistic world. The gnostic movement posed as the bearer of a secret tradition stemming from Christ, or from the Apostles. Its principal representatives, who may be considered as the successors of that Simon Magus mentioned in the New Testament, are Basilides, Valentinus, Carpocrates, and Marcion—four dark and powerful figures analogous to the four Evangelists. In this tetralogy Marcion, like St John, stands somewhat apart, as I shall show.

As a first approximation, one might say that the doctrine of the gnostics brought two innovations—one in the *form*, the other in the *matter* or content of faith. The former gave the doctrine its name. All gnostics in effect agree that the faith of 'ordinary' Christians, the common faith of the faithful, is not the limit to which initiation can attain, nor is it a sufficient condition for salvation and life eternal. It needed to be completed, to be replaced by a true science (the root word of *gnosis* meant true knowledge to the Greeks). That 'science' made the Christian knowing, *gnostic*, spiritual, a *'pneumaticus'*; it gave him a higher knowledge that saved him. It is not difficult to see that this way of dividing the faithful into two groups and of reserving perfection to the initiates changed the Christian outlook, undermined the discipline, and cast doubt upon the universality of the Church. Gnosticism attacked the very essence of the message: the idea of the Good News proclaimed to all.

Gnosticism also corrupted the essence of doctrine. It attacked the religion of love at the point where it is forever vulnerable: the

51

existence of evil. Had Jesus conquered evil? Can we believe in Jesus, Son of God, and yet accept within and all around us the shattering and undeniable fact of evil? The principle of the gnostic answer is to relieve God of all responsibility for evil, by various procedures whose basic outlines I shall presently describe.

Now that the end of the twentieth century is drawing closer, these few words will suffice to convince the reader that gnosticism still has currency, to make us realize that it lives on, concealed or else unconsciously, in not a few minds of the present.

But we must also note that in most of the ancient treatises, and even in the works of Harnack, Duchesne, and Cerfaux, the passages that deal with gnosticism spread out before us an array of absurd and extravagant doctrines, and read like a catalogue of theological monstrosities. Even the famous second *Ennead*, the treatise which the Greek philosopher Plotinus wrote against the gnostics in about 210, gives that impression of rambling. Every time the subject of the gnostics comes up, Plotinus seems to leave behind the realm of solid experience and reason, and to enter into a world of dreams, not to say nightmares: it is like listening to a psychoanalysis. Albert Rivaud was unable to see in gnosticism anything more than a degenerate syncretism. Our principal sources, the refutations of gnosticism written by the Church Fathers, take the same view. Both ancient and more recent studies of gnosticism make us despair of the human mind; they make us wonder whether there is not a close connection between intelligence and extravagance; and they hardly explain how the Church could have been so gravely endangered by lucubrations of that sort.

Within the last few years we have learned to form a more intelligent notion of these so very unintelligent ideas. Occultists, theosophists, psychoanalysts, surrealists, phenomenologists, and existentialists have compelled us to pay attention to the mythical images, the structures that inhabit the unconscious. The last two decades have given back to human thought all of that imaginary side which 'reason' had banished from it and left to poetry or magic. A phenomenologist will adjudge nothing as absurd. Nothing amazes us. We ascribe a meaning to anything, as long as someone has thought it made sense to him—more sense, at times, than his own.

Besides, the investigation has broadened. Instead of being taken for a 'heresy' peculiar to Christianity, gnosticism has come to be recognized as a general phenomenon, now that most of the great religions have revealed their gnostic movements: Manichaeism among the Persians, hermeticism among the Greeks, the Ismailites in Islam, the Jewish Kabbalah, medieval alchemy, the theosophy of the Romantics, modern occultism, and contemporary surrealism.

And finally, as though some playful demon wanted to encourage these delightful, diabolic studies, the halls of Upper Egypt in 1949 have yielded up a rich gnostic library, a veritable treasure trove for modern students of heresy, which has resulted in the publication of a heretofore unknown gnostic gospel.

I said that the interest which exegetes, philosophers, and religious historians take in gnosticism is doubtless due, in spite of their chaste silence, to the analogy between modern motifs and gnostic motifs. One is reminded of the remark of Serge Hutin that gnosticism is 'a religious ideology which always tends to reappear in Europe and the Mediterranean world in times of social and political crisis'. Should we go one step further and, with Jung, Cornelis, and Leonard, speak of 'Eternal Gnosis'?

I said earlier that I think of every 'great heresy' as having a latent existence in the structure and the depth of the human mind: at any rate, that is what this book hopes to show. It is interesting to note that in the last two decades students of heresy and phenomenologists seem agreed to admit gnosticism, which generally had been thought of as a phantasm, into the company of types and motifs. Gnosis, they seem to say, is an absurd dream, to be sure, yet it is expressive of collective man; like dream analysis it may allow us to penetrate into the depth of the operations of the human mind.[1]

In short, we have learned to take the gnostics very seriously.

[1]Several books on the subject have recently been published. 'A bibliography will be found in Serge Hutin, *Les Gnostiques* (1958), and H. Cornelis and A. Leonard, *La Gnose Eternelle* (1959). See also H. C. Puech, *La Gnose et le Temps* (1952). I also mention my own study of thirty years ago, *Le Temps et L'Eternité chez Plotin et Saint Augustin* (1933).

They are dedicated men. Their number is legion,[1] their specula-
tions are abstruse. We shall come back to them presently. But
first I shall try to do them justice, by presenting the gnostic
systems in a way that makes them convincing, meaningful, and
attractive.

Our most foolish dreams may be thought of as if they were
the transposition, into a dimension of disjointed time made up of
moments that do not hang together, of an idea that in our
normal, historical, continuous time proceeds logically, as long as
cause produces effect, and effect becomes cause in turn. In our
effort to understand the man who is cast into the unreal and
absurd by that fragmentation of time which occurs in dreams, it
will be useful to start from the reasonable, logical man, whose
nightmare is suspense and degradation.

Let us think of a mind driven out of his wits by the existence
of evil, precisely as St Augustine may have been during the period
when he, a man of genius, adhered to that form of gnosticism
branching off from the Persian religion which is known as the
Manichaean sect. At that time, Augustine was a sinner in the
flesh, and felt that his will was entirely powerless. With St Paul,
he saw struggling in himself two laws in conflict—an experience
known to all men in some degree and to spiritual natures more
than others because their aspirations are set higher. There are
many kinds of evil, no doubt, but the inner evil of temptation and
failure is the most strangulating of them all which lends
poignancy to any observations we may make about exterior evils.
A mind that is tortured by the existence of evil, that is struggling
to throw off the bondage of his sins, struggling to find an explanation for cosmic evil, or to make sense of the eternal evil of the
damned which is a mystery past understanding, that mind will
reach a point where he, like Job, demands an accounting from
the free Author of all things.

At that point, if we want to relieve Supreme Goodness of the

[1]St Epiphanius (died 403) opens his work against heresies with a list of the
sects related to gnosticism, listing them like the species of the genus: Simonians,
Menandrians, Satornilians, Basilidians, Nicolaitans, Stratiotics, Phibionites,
Saccheans, Borborites, Barbelognostics, Carpocratians, Cerinthians, Na-
zarenes, Valentinians, Ptolemaeans, Marcosians, Ophites, Cainites, Sethites,
Archontici, Cerdonians, Marcionites, Apellians, Encratites, Adamites,
Melchisecians, etc.

responsibility of having created or permitted evil, there is no alternative but to admit that that Goodness, even though infinite, was powerless to prevent the existence of evil; that there exists some dark necessity, some eternal defeat of the All-Powerful.

This, now, amounts to saying that there are two principles of being. One is the cause of good. The other, different from the first, is the cause of evil. In other words, there are two gods, or what amounts to the same thing, there is under the government of the Good God some Demiurge, uncontrollable and in his own domain sovereign, who creates evil. And since creation as a whole contains good and evil inextricably intermingled, with evil predominating, we are quickly brought to the view that God has no authority in 'creation', which has been started and is now ruled over by an evil Demiurge.

Here we are caught in the blind alley of the absurd axiom that admits two sovereign principles, one of good, the other of evil. I may perhaps reduce the absurdity by making of that principle of evil not so much a second God, forever equal and opposed to the first principle, but rather an active devil. Or, if I am a philosopher, I may at any rate turn him into a principle of degradation, a necessity of decay and fall, presumably inherent in the act of creation much like the stringing out of words and syllables is a necessity of speech. In other words, without dividing God in two, we can reduce his responsibility by turning it into something like an indirect and inevitable consequence of creation —a *compossible*, Leibniz would have said.

This hypothesis is burdensome. But how it sets me free! I am no longer shocked in the face of evil. I am no longer the sole and secret cause of the evil within me, since even God Himself to some degree suffers the same constraint of evil, and carries within Him, too, the necessity of fall and separation. In the extreme, I can say with St Augustine that 'it is not I who sins, but I do not know what evil nature that is within me'. My metaphysics absolves me of the accusations of my moral sense: it is impossible for me not to do evil. As for the evil outside me, that is the work not of the All-Powerful and All-Perfect, but of a fated law of degradation.

Nor is this all. The doctrine gives me incomparable bliss, the possession of eternity anticipated. In fact, the doctrine is the clear and easy way that I must follow from now on to achieve salvation, the way by which I shall return into that Good God from Whom I have come, Who is the source of all my goodness, in Whom I will be one with what is eternal in me. For evil is not a part of me, and at heart I remain unstained. I am separated from God only by the interval of creation, not by the distance of sin. In other words, I am not separated really and basically. To become one with God I do not need to convert since I am not corrupted, I need not even come back since I am not apart. I only need to remember, remember once more what is my eternal condition. I am always in the light.

That salvation toward which I am tending, which ordinary Christians imagine to be far off, uncertain, elusive, and depending on merit, is not outside of me but within me. I need not run the risk of losing it, because I have it. All I need do is to become aware of this eternal fact. Instead of the effort of hoping for salvation, I now shall take my rest in recalling its possession. Instead of the effort of faith, I now have a clear *knowledge, gnosis*. That is the meaning of gnosticism.

The system is logical. Its tremendous psychic advantages are apparent. True, it requires setting up this axiom which subjects God to necessity, in other words, to give evil the advantage over good, and to make of evil, in the sense of the necessity of the fall, the true God and master even over God Himself. But in return for accepting this absurdity, I can relieve man of the burden of evil and assure him of salvation. In place of the painful effort of sacrifice, I now have an act of knowing which makes me one with the purity of my eternal essence.

The system is enduring. It inspires the mysticism of Plotinus, and the metaphysics of Spinoza. It reappears somewhat more veiled in the abstract gnosticism of post-Kantian philosophy, especially Hegel's. Perhaps this system of salvation by knowledge is not alien even to Buddhist illumination. We meet it again in all those splintering doctrines which project God as far as possible from the world, into an ineffable transcendence; which are no longer troubled to see the world subjected to necessity and discord, the 'eternal return', and war.

The system may seem strange, even unthinkable. But on reflection, is there an alternative for those who are not atheists and yet cannot believe, as Jews and Christians believe, that God in His freedom allows freedom to evil? St Irenaeus, writing against the gnostics called 'heretics', already clearly set forth this three-fold logical sequence: if we reject both the gnostics' separation of God and the world, and the pantheistic fusion of God with the world—the first because it renders God unthinkable, the second because it compels him by necessity to create evil— there is only one answer left, the Christian and reasonable answer.[1]

These were the main traits and the central axis of the system. They hold no surprises for the modern reader. The scene is familiar. We may even have the strange impression of having read these sequences before in novels, essays, or works of philosophy of recent years, though surely there can be no question of any direct influence. We cannot imagine Gide, Sartre, or Georges Bataille seeking inspiration in Basilides, Marcion, Valentinus, or Carpocrates. If there is an analogy between our contemporaries and the gnostics, it is because gnosticism, far from being a passing aberration, stems from a fundamental attitude of the human mind in the face of the problem of being, and of Christianity. That attitude is, I believe, what I have called dissociation.[2]

It consists in an unflagging refusal ever to accept the fact that in temporal existence form mingles with matter, the pure with the impure, eternity with time. It means to make use of the intellect in order to imagine oneself all-pure, wholly free and already eternal—and to leave all the rest to the realms of becoming, the imagination, fatality, all those inferior and irrational varieties of nothingness. Such a way of thinking, I believe, always has existed, exists now, and always will exist. For Plato it was a temptation, which he overcame; in Aristotle, a weakness; with Philo, a doctrine; with Plotinus, a mystical metaphysics; to Spinoza, an ethics, that is, a system of salvation; to Hegel, a dialectical logic; in our day, finally, it inspired calamitous 'moral systems' like Gide's, and those of several of our existentialists.

Applied to Christianity, that turn of mind leads to a denial of the historical element, and of development in time. In particular it leads to a dissociation of the symbolic and mythical

[1]*Adversus Haereses*, II, 30   [2]*Existence temporelle*, pp. 75-103

Christ, who is timeless, known to faith, and alone sufficient and necessary, from the historical man of Nazareth, who is in time and known from the reports of his contemporaries. That is, it turns the Incarnation into something that thought cannot encompass. We shall meet the same difficulty, and the same dissociation in Arius, Nestorius, and many thinkers of the present, from Loisy to Goguel or Bultmann.

The gnostics offer the advantage of showing how this way of thinking tends toward a crude, faceless, monstrous condition, without any precaution or intellectual disguise, in a frenzy of oriental imagery: they offer a spectacular diversity of doctrines sprung from the same need, yet without any direct influence on one another—while the various western philosophies descend from one another and maintain their dialogue. With the gnostics, we find ourselves in the fantastic world of dreamers. They all sleep in the same room, but their dreams do not touch one another.

I cannot here sketch the various systems—they defy a summing up. If we must have parallels, it could be said that Basilides —a logical mind who had about him, in Renan's words, 'a certain sadness, a gloomy, glacial resignation'—reminds us of Hegel. Valentinus would then be Schelling, more of a poet, more intuitive, and imbued with love. Valentinus's system could be compared to that which Plotinus was to develop later. His answer to difficult questions was: 'You will forever remain simple believers.' And his disciples at such moments would knit their brows and only say: 'Oh Profundity!' In a recent book some of the basic traits of Valentinus's system are described as follows:

'The Valentinian world is subject to rules that are essentially "sacramental". Every plane of existence draws its life, in a sacramental mode, from the life that descends from the next higher plane. But only those beings are capable of grasping the "sacramental" value of the forms on their own plane, whose secret nature, in reality a stranger to the plane on which it finds itself, unconsciously aspires toward rejoining that higher plane which is its own.

'At the highest point of Valentinus's Pleroma stands the nameless Father, Pro-Pater, whom we have met before. He constitutes a pair, or syzygy, with his own Secret Thought, which is inseparable from him to a point where he may be thought of as androgynous. This Thought bears several significant names. It is called Ennoia, or thought enacted, but is called also by the name *Sige* or Silence and *Charis* or Grace. From this first pair there emanates a second, consisting of Monogenes and Truth. The function of Monogenes is to reunite within himself the attributes of unity and of multiplicity. He is Divine thought in the act of communication, and endows all beings with their truth. These first four Aeons form a Tetrad which, by the law of reflection, divides into an Ogdoad. The four male elements of Ogdoad also constitute a Tetrad. From the syzygy Monogenes-Truth emanates the pair Logos-Life, whose Johannine derivation is undeniable. The Logos, third of the male Aeons, bears a plainly creative aspect, born out by the name of his companion spirit, Life of the Pleroma, of which the "lives" of the other planes are reduced images. The Logos contributes in a special way to the emission of the pleromatic Christ, a synthetic entity combining within itself the influx of all the Aeons, and from which in turn emanates the Savior, who will issue from the Pleroma to "form" Achamoth, corrupted Wisdom. The last two Aeons are called Anthropos and Ekklesia, Man and Election (Election rather than Church, because it is precisely the Idea of predestination to life in the Pleroma). This last female Aeon has a number of aspects, of which the most important is Sophia.

'All the Aeons of the Pleroma are filled with desire to pierce the mystery of the Father hidden in the bosom of Silence. But their desire, enlightened by the Intellect, remains within the bounds of what is permitted. Only Sophia's urge is inordinate. This is because Sophia does, in fact, have the function of the Idea of the Soul within the bosom of the Pleroma, and it is in the nature of the soul to be ruled by *horme*, impulsiveness. The urge of Sophia, in its unlimited and indefinite—that is, formless— aspect threatened to overthrow the whole structure of the Pleroma because Sophia, lost in the infinite sweetness of the Father, could find no fixed abode. But at this point the other Aeons emitted a special Entity, destined to stabilize the Pleroma that had been shaken by the "passions" of Sophia. That Entity is called *Horos*, or *Stauros*, the Limiter or the Cross-stake. This Limiter excludes from the Pleroma everything contrary to its immutable nature. It is the type of every "judgment", which is expressed by the cross. It bears a special relation to the Logos which also possesses a dividing power. As the Limiter divides, it also holds together, in keeping with the twofold meaning of the word *stauros*, stake; instrument of punishment, and marker of the enclosure.'

Carpocrates, who lived in Alexandria, was an immoralist. He understood all the possibilities. He understood particularly that if the soul is merely banished within the flesh, and the flesh is not myself, then the flesh may gratify all its appetites without doing wrong. Once you are on that incline it is hard to stop. Mysticism and sensuality become identified, and each supports the other, both being boundless. In the end debauchery becomes the means to free the spirit as well as the flesh. Women belonged to all, like the light of day. Carpocrates cannot be blamed for his cynical logic: he merely drew the consequences. Whether he practised what he thought permissible we shall never know.

One thing is incontestable. The problems of sex, generally wrapped in silence and left to haunt man, were brought out into broad daylight by the gnostics. The gnostics tried to exorcise sex by sublimating it. Quite often the secret of their cosmogony is a divine copulation. At times, perversions of the flesh are taken for means to humble the body, to make it realize its disgrace, as though by sinning man made himself clean. Sex is generally condemned when it leads to procreation. Marriage is considered imperfect—not, however, the *sacred marriage*. In some instances, gnosticism worshipped woman as 'pneumatic and pure, pleroma of pleromas'. The Valentinians believed that the soul, who is female even in man, is searching for her counterpart, a male angel with whom she will form the complete being. Gnosticism invented a cult of the 'eternal feminine'. It fused the feminine Wisdom of the Mother with the Holy Spirit. These are motifs we shall meet elsewhere.

But let us leave such matters to the philosophers, and consider how this dualistic system on the one hand, and on the other Jewish monotheism and the Christian mystery, could live side by side. To all appearances the two repel each other. But then comes history and shows us that, alas, anything will combine with anything. The world abounds with mongrel breeds.

It could be held that even Greek philosophy already achieved that strange symbiosis: Plato and Aristotle both recognized the existence of an opposition to the principle of order, which they called multiplicity, space, necessity, formless matter. Which comes down to setting up for all eternity two opposing gods.

However, among the Jews of Alexandria the soil was prepared to receive such mixtures. Philo, who lived at the same time as Jesus but did not know him, raised God beyond all quality: God was so high that he could not be thought of with our concepts, not even the most pure. He acts upon his creation through intermediary agents that allow him to remain pure; the principal such agent is the Logos. He has organized the universe out of formless matter. In the matter so organized by the *logos*, there exist pure elements, a kind of captive atoms. Prophets and wise men carry such atoms of purity within them. In the course of their lives they set them free, helped by the Word, helped always by asceticism and sometimes by ecstasy. We have no way of knowing where in his structure Philo would have placed Jesus; possibly as a cosmic mediator between the cosmos and the Unreachable.

But, by contrast, we know well the reasoning of the gnostics. They were furious logicians, and poets and magicians to boot, rather than mystics. Once they were launched they did not stop again. Above all, they know full well the power of radical and obstinate negation. God has no relation to the world and its history. He is an 'alien God', radically *other*, hidden, unnameable, unknown except by revelation, totally *new* if he manifests himself beneath himself. Opposed to him is either a weak, mean, stupid Demiurge, or else the devil himself, unbegotten principle, accursed god, prince of darkness, upon whom rests the burden of original sin or the curse—a god known only too well. This second god condemns us to existence within time. The first god sets us free of it forever, through knowledge.

I said that this form of thought had its origin in the consciousness of evil. It carries the sensitivity to evil to its utmost extreme. The gnostics do not limit themselves to moral evil, or even cosmic evil: the very *existence in time* is to them the evil *per se*.

The gnostic feels that the human condition is precarious, paradoxical, and unworthy. He grieves that he is bound by the law, by death, by fate, and more: by the fall, disgrace, defilement.

Marcion, for example, likes to describe men as begotten in an obscene deed, thrown out into the world by grotesque convulsions, a sack of excrement which in the end will be dissolved by death. Valentinus took pleasure in describing the human condition as the place of deep sadness, nausea, and the sudden terror that grips us—states far beyond mere anguish because we do not know their meaning. Think only, he says, of the fact of birth, in spite of all appearances every bit as absurd as death, and yet so readily condoned, so foolishly celebrated . . . Birth which we suffer from our parents without having wanted it, which we perversely and willingly give to others—birth is the entry into a condition that would be true damnation if death and Jesus did not deliver us from it. The Buddhists go too far, no doubt, when they subject human destinies to transmigration, a 'pouring into new vessels' which goes on into infinity because Christ does not reincarnate himself. But they have rightly understood that history is a 'growth of death'. What is time? Time is the space of free fall. It stems from a first fall, a primal disaster, which could be ascribed to God because the Supreme Wisdom had relinquished *fulness*. If we prefer to ascribe it to man, we say that time was born when Primordial Man was snatched up by Darkness.

We are not far from the Christian mystery. The truth of that mystery is indeed borne out by the fact that it may be approached from an anterior myth. That famous agony of Jesus —is it not the exemplary experience, fittingly called crucial, of that damnation which is existence in time? Each moment of our lives is virtually a passion. The wrong done by Adam and Eve explains how sentence was passed that there be time; it unleashes history which rushed from it in a landslide of failures. Time is the crumbling of the worlds.

Biblical history is called to witness. Scripture not only puts before us these demoniac powers that rule heaven and earth, but gives a detailed recital of these lawless times when the evil principle is master, the wicked Demiurge called Jehovah. This raging God who punished a whole race for the sin of the first pair of lovers; who, still worse, saves of the whole accursed race only

Gnosticism

one single family; who demands blood sacrifice, commands wars of extermination, who ties his people to a body of laws that are practically impossible to follow, and so force his people either into hypocrisy or into obsession: how could that God lay claim to God's essential quality, infinite goodness and love?

This gnostic attack on the Old Testament strikes a responding chord among the Christians. It explains why for so long the Church has not recommended the reading of the Bible to lay people of little learning, and why the ancient theologians laid so much stress on allegorical exegesis while playing down or avoiding altogether the difficulties of history. We know today that God is a patient teacher. He will allow peoples and civilizations to retain their pristine mentality for a long time. He raised up prophets in Israel to set that mentality right little by little. And his power and kindness are manifest in his choice of the hardest, the most inflexible of peoples. Yet in spite of the *allegory* of the ancients and the *development* of the moderns the difficulty remains, and we still feel at times the opposition between the 'Avenging God' and the Heavenly Father. We may wonder whether we did not complaisantly blur the vast difference between the God of the Jews, Creator and Law-giver, and the absolute Love revealed by the sole Jesus Christ. However that may be, gnosticism took full advantage of the impression produced within us by the Christian juncture. St Paul, even while he retained his Jewish temperament, had already gone quite far in his diatribe against the 'Law' of his people. Gnosticism went far beyond Paul. It can be said that gnosticism wielded the axe with insolence, and dealt two intolerable blows. Horizontally, it severed Jewish history and Christian history in a radical cleavage, condemned Moses and Abraham, and looked on Jesus as the founder of the new age. Vertically—and that was worse and plainly unthinkable for a Jew or a Christian, nay even a Greek—it set up in heaven the opposition between a Good Father and a Wicked Creator.

At first sight, there was no doctrine more disconsolate. Gnosticism such as I have described it seems to be the metaphysics of despair. But we may not trust first sights, and must greatly distrust the cunning of despair.

At this point I wish to make an observation that seems to me

63

of the first importance, and to which I shall refer more than once in our study of the dialectics of the great systems of religious thought.

By force of being separated, the extremes touch. Contrasting errors, which one would suppose to be hostile to each other, secretly cross-breed and strengthen one another. Like an electric current the mind alternates almost instantaneously from one to the other. In this unconscious oscillation and immediate compensation, the human mind imagines it achieves balance—in fact, it makes a mockery of balance: as though a plumb line, unable to hang straight, were in its helplessness and impatience to turn itself into a pendulum.

If I think of God as being beyond all being and all knowledge, I will tend to take the world for my possession. Better still, I will think of myself as not accountable for all my over-sensuous and violent dealings. I vaguely realize that a Being whom I do not know, and who does not know me, can take no real interest in what goes on in a world that is to him like a dream. In such a world, my knowledge rejoices in finding nothing but necessity, my instincts nothing but freedom. There is a very lively, though hidden, tie between certain doctrines of absolute transcendence, and rationalism or immoralism. We shall see it soon, when we turn to Islam.

Among the gnostics, the law of compensation operates with special power. With them, despair is of a piece with the certainty of bliss, the bliss of certainty. The gnostic, as I said, cherishes the hallucination of defilement, which is quite the contrary of the consciousness of sin. For defilement is essentially like a spot on a garment, it is outside of myself, while sin is within me, in that my conscience feels that I must answer for my actions. I note in passing that the success of psychoanalysis is due to the fact that it tends to transform a sin into a stain, confession into riddance, the examination of conscience into an analysis of the contents of consciousness, the confessor into a physician: psychoanalysis *gnosticizes*. I vomit my defect, and no longer acknowledge it. This remark may help a modern man understand the attraction of transforming a sin into a stain, by whatever process. The more I stress the external, involuntary, sticky, viscous character of my failure, the more I bring out my own remoteness from the stain, my inviolable purity. Being locked up is altogether different from being guilty. The gnostic can be soiled, stained: but he is not at fault nor impure, on the contrary. As his consciousness of his defilement grows, so does the knowledge of his purity. And at the very moment when he condemns existence he proclaims, or rather undergoes, his separation from this evil of being, for he is that being no longer. The sentence he pronounces upon the evil from which he excludes himself, that same sentence pronounces him pure. Even more, it lets him achieve salvation by knowledge, *gnosis.*

In this way out of the extreme of pessimism is born the absolute extreme of optimism, eternal bliss. The exaggerations of the gnostics show the process with great clarity. But I believe the same game is being played in every form of pessimism. Desperate men hang themselves. The pessimists have gone on living.

A gnostic poem, reported by E. Beneviste and H. C. Puech,[1] will serve as an example:

> Born of light and of the gods
> I am in exile and cut off from them.
> The enemies who have covered me
> Have carried me off among the dead.
> May he be blessed and find deliverance
> Who will deliver my soul from anguish!
> I am a god, and born of gods,
> Shining, sparkling, luminous,
> Radiant, perfumed and beautiful,
> But henceforth reduced to suffering.

'You are immortal from the beginning,' declares Valentinus. The true gnostic, in one and the same act of knowledge, experiences his (accidental) fall and his (essential) salvation. He has the knowledge, nay the certitude—which is more than the hope—that he is in possession of the absolute truth, of total knowledge. He holds within himself that illumination which predestines him for salvation unconditionally and without preparation in time. He need not become perfect, grow, mature, run the risks of freedom, fall and pick himself up, or ask for

[1] Fragment of Turfan M 7 in *Sitzungsberichte der Preussischen Akademie der Wissenschaften,* 1934, pp. 874-5.

forgiveness. Salvation is not a conversion of the will by the acceptance of time, but an illumination of the intellect which reveals to him that he has never been in time, except as its prisoner. But there is Christ who has chosen him, and who will in a moment deliver him from this nightmare of existence.

That salvation by the intellect regenerates him, unifies him, enlightens him and makes him godlike. It identifies him with that part of him which is eternal, authentic, incorporeal. This is true liberation. The gnostic can enjoy even now complete freedom in every respect. He is above the laws and above good and evil, independent of the creator and the judge. He is indifferent, unimpeachable. He possesses a *bythos exousias*, an abyss of freedom. He has been saved, by his gnosis not his works, and he is saved whatever he may do. Gold remains gold even when it falls into the muck. In fact, this total freedom which allows him either to abstain from all desire, or to surrender to desire and indulge the flesh to the limit, is reserved for those who are perfect, who have the Spirit, for the *pneumatici*. As for the *psychici*, who have the soul but not the Spirit, they must educate themselves in time, by effort and good works.

Jesus is the Savior in the sense that he reveals, illumines, and teaches by example. It is no longer absolutely necessary that his acts have historical reality. Their saving virtue lies in their symbolic and exemplary, timeless value. This view differs sharply from that of the faithful. For them, Jesus truly lived, he is truly dead and risen. He submitted to the ultimate bondage of time, entered into a human family, was born of Mary. For Marcion, Jesus springs into being all at once, thirty years old, *subito filius et subito missus et subito Christus*, without antecedents, a phantom and imaginary Savior who appears without having really become flesh. His passion and resurrection might be mere illusions. Basilides thought that someone else had suffered on the cross in place of Jesus. For the rest, our resurrection is not something for which we have to wait. It has occurred already, in baptism. Historic time is thus denied, replaced by a mythical and timeless time.

Marcion came next. He was a practical man, impetuous, inquiring, a man of the sea as were Pelagius and Lamennais, a bishop's son, and versed in money matters. He brought the various scattered motifs together, simplified what had grown too luxuriant, westernized the influences of oriental magic, and made official what had been underground. Instead of adding one more school of thought, he set up a Church. It was clear to him that to succeed he had to go to Rome. In fact, he had made a present of two hundred sesterces to the Roman community.

At first a zealous Catholic, he became infatuated with an excessively simple idea, and could not find his way out of the interlocking consequences that flowed from it. Marcion took up one aspect of St Paul's vast thought structure, as Luther did later, and carried it to infinite extremes. Jehovah, God of the Jews, had patently failed with his Jewish methods that consisted in promising a masterful Messiah. God's goodness had appeared in Jesus who is Love, something which only Paul had understood. Marcion based love upon the cross. He preached asceticism in food and drink and sexual abstinence. Husband and wife had to separate before they could receive baptism. He wanted to pierce through the Judaic corruptions that still remained in the Church, and to recover the hard, pure diamond, Jesus alone. He purged the gospels, even that of St Luke, and the epistles, even those of St Paul, of everything that Judaized and by that token of all that humanized Jesus. Without birth, without growth, without suffering, without final agony—entirely appearance and apparition— Jesus now became a religious myth. There are to this day men who feel that Marcion was the real Christian. Couchoud said to me more than o. ;e: 'Marcion saw clear. Everything is true in the *Credo* except the words "under Pontius Pilate".' Those who with Bultmann would 'demythologize' the gospel are Marcion's spiritual children.

The wide-spread and rapid success of Marcion's Church is astounding. It produced many men of holiness and many martyrs, and shook the foundations of the ecclesiastic order. It was as anti-Semitic as it was anti-Greek; the new Christians, conscious of their newness, felt the need to define themselves in contrast to the others. Marcion's Church was Roman in its warlike and violent crudity, its primal spirit. It courted the absolute by its horror of all compromises and concessions to flesh and blood. Above all, it seemed to simplify simplicity itself, and to reveal the secret of the gospel. The word NEW came fully into its own. In this one word is summed up the great enterprise, the second conversion in the midst of life, and the discovery of a new Church, pure at last!

The historians of Marcion's time lay stress upon the rôle he played in the development of the Church. They underline the danger that Marcion's organization constituted: it might have turned the second generation of the Church into Marcionites from one day to the next, almost before they knew it. But nothing is more fruitful for a young and growing Church than a clear danger. The threat turns into a source of strength. Until Marcion came, the Church could almost disregard those innovators and eccentrics of the kind that every religious society throws off. By causing irritation on the danger spots they represent, they prompt the sharpening of doctrinal definitions; they strengthen the union of the faithful when it grows slack in the intervals between persecutions. But Marcion was the first to organize a counter-Church, with a counter-Scripture, a more exacting morality, and blood witnesses: to the Marcionites martyrdom was the true birth, the escape toward love.

An official list of inspired scriptures of apostolic origin had existed, of course, before Marcion. But Marcion's omissions and manipulations made it an absolute necessity to fix the text of these writings—to make of them, as it were, a true copy. Since Marcion had taken liberties, in order to make disappear whatever he judged discordant, the great Church was compelled to set the gospels down side by side—rather than making them agree, and become synoptic the way Tatian did. This fact is of great value to modern exegesis which thrives on discordances, those proofs of an invisible harmony. Thus Marcion promoted the publication of the Book of books, authentic, multiple and one.

There had been bishops before Marcion, guardians of the unity of faith. But after him, the bishops were more certain that they were necessary, and they were more united. After Marcion and gnosticism, there was a true episcopate.

There had been traditions in each of the Churches before gnosticism and Marcion. But from then on these traditions—in the main lists of succession and of traditional beliefs—were understood more profoundly as the expressions of a Tradition. And, in complete contrast to the gnostic secrets that had been passed on in the lodges of the initiates since Jesus, Tradition was now understood as a stream of lasting vitality, a rule of faith 'kept young by the Church'. The phrase is that of St Irenaeus, who used it in Lyons where he had come from Asia toward the end of the second century. Irenaeus was the man who had spoken to men who had spoken to the Apostles, and was not in vain called the Conciliator.

And after gnosticism the Church, assembled in what was virtually a nameless Council, became fully aware of God's nearness to man in conscious contrast to gnosticism. God was not in the distant heavens; the creature was his own immediate handiwork, his sign, the word bespeaking his presence. The Old Testament was not the antithesis of the New but its pre-history, for history was one unbroken stream. Lastly, Christ was no stranger to history. In him the Word had become flesh and so had transfigured all matter. The refutation of gnosticism lent to Catholicism of the late second century a complexion that is very modern.

Montanism

We recall here the Montanist movement which in a sense foreshadows modern times.

'Maranatha!—The Lord is coming!' was the call of the earliest Christians, a part of the liturgy which may have expressed the hope that the Savior would return in glory during the *agape* meal, the 'love feast'. The thought of imminence dominated the whole generation, which was expecting eternity to begin perhaps this very evening. Faith still holds to that expectation, although up to the atomic age the slow pace of history has compelled us to postpone it constantly.

However, the dialectic of salvation seemed to men of education to be still incomplete. The Father had shown himself in the Old Testament, the Son in the New. Through St John had come the promise of the Spirit closing the circle of eternity, who would console and reveal. And one could no doubt hold the belief that Pentecost, and the first preaching of the gospel, had fulfilled John's prophecy. But one might also believe that that had been merely an announcement, that the kingdom of the Spirit would come in the end, and that one would see eternity ruling in time, the kingdom of the Spirit here on earth. This eternal-temporal dream has haunted many minds. The perfect city in a time that has stopped moving is the Marxist myth. Such was the idea the 'this-worldly' Jews had of the Messiah. Jesus had not satisfied that expectation because 'his kingdom was not of this world'. But that, too, could be considered a mere delay, after which he would complete his work.

In the village of Ardabau, lost somewhere in Cyrene, visions came to Montanus, an aged priest of Cybele, and two women, Maximilia and Priscilla. This in itself was not extraordinary. But we note that these new prophets, in contrast to the prophets of the Bible, speak in a state of ecstasy, as though their personality were suspended while the Paraclete speaks in them. The Spirit announces the return of Jesus, and the coming of the new Jerusalem which will lie between Tymion and Pepuza, Phrygian towns. The three attracted a crowd of followers. Marriages are dissolved, property is communized. The movement meets with remarkable success in the East. Pepuza becomes a holy place. The sect desires its own martyrs, and the wish comes true.

Montanism touched Rome and the fervent Church of Lyons, in Gaul, whose martyrs intervened to protect the movement against condemnation. St Irenaeus, the great opponent of gnosticism and of Marcion, long remained undecided about the Montanists. Tertullian, always attracted to extremes, rallied to Montanism: a genius of the early centuries turned Catharist. Before his conversion to Montanism, Tertullian had recommended fasting—he now makes it a duty. He had allowed the readmission of Christians who had fallen into sin—he now bars them. He had allowed believers to flee from persecution—now he demands that they expose themselves to it. He had advised widows not to remarry—he now forbids re-marriage under pain of adultery. Tertullian's history shows that headlong decline we often find in religious minds, among them Lamennais. The modernity of Montanism is unmistakable. Newman has said that Montanus, with his fastings and his air of innocence regained, was an 'unpleasant anticipation of St Francis of Assisi'.

Montanus had succeeded even in making it an occasion of

joy to give up one's life. The famous report of the martyrs of Lyons has a ring of happiness. Blandinus's bliss in the midst of torture seemed to make him insensitive to pain. Montanist groups gave the impression of paradisiac delight. But Rome was the first to see that this new prophecy would step by step endanger the entire setting of the faith of that time, that it would endanger the Church and religious training. Montanism, more perhaps even than Marcionism, is the prototype of that religious illusion which is caused by the extreme resemblance on first sight between Catharist purity and patient saintliness.

Montanism is our first sight of the impatient Christian who must have the Spirit in utter purity, and total and immediate perfection without submitting to the servitudes of institution or of time. The Montanist experience and the case of Tertullian have given us much to think about.

After Montanism there emerges a Church that lays stress on its *institutional* side as we would say today, more than on its prophetic side which we would call today the manifestation of the event. Ever since Montanus the Church has distrusted prophets. But let us note also that the laity, now less responsible for the life of the Church, became freer to follow its own ways. The Church had been a bride to the Montanists; it now became more like a mother to the laity. In fact, the pressures and counter-pressures of the Montanist crisis begin to define the meaning of 'laity'. That crisis stripped the layman of the prophetic function, and incorporated him more firmly into the hierarchical community, in somewhat passive submission. But the memory of the danger, which was to emerge again in the Catharist crisis, has also given rise among the hierarchy, and later the religious orders, to a certain attitude of defiance toward the laity. The Church had reason to distrust unauthorized and uncontrollable prophets, still more prophetic women. The true prophet will from now on be a member of a religious order, a Catharist loyal to the Church, a layman regulated by the Church.

Besides, after Montanism the Church can no longer consider herself as the receptacle of pure souls only. The danger of that notion has become too clear. She grows into a Church that accepts being a mixture. But the pure within the Church feel the duty to purify the less pure and to raise them to their own level, and so the Church after the Montanist crisis awakens more fully to her teaching function. She does not cast out sinners, but by discipline and the practice of progressive purification she undertakes to educate the low man to a middling, the middling to a perfect state, and even the saint to a condition of still greater perfection. Nothing is ever an assured possession, nothing is ever lost.

Gnostics and Montanists are alike in that both tried to be something more than the great, vast Church. The former tried to be more intelligent, in their extreme form to be the only intelligent believers. The latter tried to be purer, in their extreme form to be the only pure ones. Attempts of that kind, I said, could be foreseen ever since the Church became world-wide and as mixed as a world inevitably is.

The history of the second century after Jesus is a preview of the future, a first notice, the shape of things to come. We can perhaps see it more clearly today, foreshortened by the distance in time.

In truth, the contrasting upheavals of maximism and of minimism were predictable. Every doctrine of balance and simplicity gives rise on the right to exaggerated rigor, and on the left to an excessive flexibility in all directions that may dissolve it. We can observe it in every order, particularly in politics and even more in a structure devoted to saintliness and truth. Both excesses can be discovered in Christianity from the very beginning. Radical Judaism is a sort of maximism against which Paul takes the field; while the Docetism of Cerinthus, who considers Jesus a mere phantom of being, represents that rationalist minimism against which the school of St John argues and preaches.

Just so, the unbelieving intellect faced with Jesus wavers, as I said elsewhere, between two negative paths: whether to turn Jesus into a deified man, or whether to turn him into a humanized myth. These are the two extremes, the two high points of the pendulum of doubt, the secret oscillation which renders the Incarnation of God's Son empty by excess or by want.

In the days of the gnostics, Judeo-Christianity already had no future. Its radical opposite, the absolute anti-Judaism of the gnostics and of Marcion, takes up all the space. The consequence of gnosticism, as I said, was to strip Jesus of his citizen's status in history, to disincarnate him and make him a thing of the imagination, or an abstraction.

As I reflect upon the history of the second crucial crisis, I grow aware of its almost inevitable nature. Catholicism had to face all the lively habits of the intellect, as did Jesus, and engage in conversation with the Tempter.

Among all the temptations of the mind the temptation of gnosticism has always seemed to me the most profound. It cuts to the very concept of salvation. It proposes to the freedom of the intellect an option which in my view is the most fundamental of them all—and which has over the centuries set against one another minds of the first order: Plotinus against St Augustine, Averroes against St Thomas, Spinoza against Pascal, Kierkegaard against Hegel, Newman against Renan, Brunschvicg against Blondel, Sartre against Marcel. That life eternal which is our goal—shall we expect to find it in time, in the form of a salvation achieved by the senses or pure freedom or dialectics? Or does time contain only the seed corn of salvation that is to blossom only in that duration past our understanding, without history and without succession, which we call eternity? The gnostics certainly did not deny survival after death. But by proposing the option under which salvation lies in the knowledge of its eternity which the mind achieves in this world, they made survival pointless. Time, no longer now the dimension of our choosing and of love, became at bottom insignificant. It was merely the devil who had subjected us to time's dark and useless illusion.

The Church reacted against gnosticism and in reacting found its strength. Several of her vital organs assumed their functions. She tested herself, stocked up her arsenal, matured, and grew.

But as we have seen in the case of Judeo-Christianity, every reaction means a limitation. It cuts short a positive development that would no doubt have been possible. In religion no less than in education, criticism and especially the suppression of an error or a mistake affect elements of life that are related to the error though distinct from it, and threaten to smother them. Even as we correct a child's fit of anger, we risk weakening his vigor. It is in order, then, to ask ourselves each time we condemn: which are the seeds, now buried once more in the soil, that will have to wait longer before they can grow up into the light? That is to say, we must seek out what was valid in gnosticism, and what counter-gnosticism kept from growing.

The literature of our day often emphasizes the presence of gnostic currents. C. G. Jung, the analytical psychologist, gave them particular attention. He compared the motifs of gnostic thought with those of dreams, in order to identify the permanent archetypes which are perhaps anterior to all positive religions. It may be held that the study of the gnostic imaginings allows us to identify the primordial images that lie buried within us. The writings of Guénon, d'Abellio, and Gurdjieff lend a new meaning to those images. We need only to read Louis Pauwels' *The Dawn of Magic*. But these affinities, if they do exist, would serve to show rather that gnosticism brings to light the infantile and fragmented chaos of the collective unconscious to which modern man, tired of reason, turns for renewal, inspiration and support. In our view, this is the infernal and perhaps demoniac element in gnosticism, the recourse to the abyss that we encounter in periods of despair such as our own. Gnosticism, it has been said, does not reveal to us the depths of God of which St Paul spoke, but informs us of the depths of man, the troubled depths out of which con-sciousness arises. Modern man is caught between the mysterious depth of God and the absurd depth of his own being. Faith gives us the first, gnosticism the second.

Still, may we not interpret gnosticism in a better sense and ask ourselves if, once it was righted or sublimated by faith, it did not contain elements that are valid? We may ask ourselves whether the necessary reaction of the Church against those disordered imaginings has not in some way helped to desiccate Western theology; whether it has not helped especially to strip faith of its importance as a way of knowing, its intellectual light; and whether, after the sad experience of abuse, we have not cast back into the shadows certain potentialities that were present in St Paul and even in St John.

St Paul spoke of an ulterior and higher knowledge attained not in separation from the common faith but in the deepening of that faith. Faith, despite its obscurity which is rather the test of our present imperfect state, is a source of light, of an embracing and full knowledge that penetrates the unseen history of every destiny and of all ages. The theology of the Greek Fathers and of the Eastern Orthodox theologians is far less anti-gnostic than is Latin and Roman theology, no doubt because it was in Rome that the Church had to face up to the risks to which the faith was exposed by such adventures. The positive spirit of the Roman clergy, the Roman popes and the bishops of Gaul expressed the response of Christian sensitivity united under authority. Later, the personal experience of St Augustine would confirm Rome and the West. We must not forget that this astounding genius, unquestionably the greatest genius in all Christianity, who gave us something like a second edition of the faith, was for nine years an ardent gnostic.

In our own day, Eternal Gnosis is very much alive and active. But it works outside of the Church, without mutual confusion or penetration. In surrealism, existentialism and theosophy modern gnosticism displays its luna-moth wings. Beneath their rainbow play of many colors the microscope reveals the unchanging structure. The danger of mystic prophecy practised by women and the laity was exorcised, I said, almost as soon as it appeared. But may it not be that the laity has suffered from that fact ever since? The theology of the Western scholastics, so little mystical and above all so little cosmic, has forced Paulinian inspiration to seek refuge in mysticism and poetry, often heterodox like that of Master Eckhardt.

In the Eastern Orthodox Church the tradition of a total knowledge that embraces both the natural and the supernatural, the cosmic and the divine mystery, has kept a stronger hold, as the works of Soloviev and Berdaev make plain. With us in the West, theology to this day has been agnostic and rational, for the same reasons which have kept the laity in the Church in a routine and passive rôle. In this way, the Catholic Church has been preserved from illuminism, and has remained in a steady light visible to all. But she has paid a price. One could wish that certain treasures that have been discarded could be found again and taken in.

The gnosticism of Marcion and Montanus, then, has left its marks on the face of the eternal Church. Like every conflict it has had its effect upon the time of the Church, retarding certain developments, and advancing, even precipitating certain forward steps. To see in Marcion the founder in reverse of the episcopate and the canon of Scripture would be a facile, though tempting, confusion. Origin is one thing, emergence another. The moment when the earth swallows a seed, and the moment when the root appears are not the same. Before the shoots can spring up in the furrow, it must rain. Heresy may at times be the outside agent that causes the appearance of what is virtually, latently there. Gnosticism so exercised its influence upon the birth of Catholic theology and mysticism, by inspiring in them certain inner fears and prompting certain precautions.

However, after so many centuries, so many changes and renewals on the face of the earth, these long exiles to which total theology or lay prophecy have fortunately been subjected, are at an end. Our ecumenical culture, our knowledge of patristics, the universal apostolate, the stock-taking of the people of God in self-appraisal, and the history of salvation now allow that what has been lost may be recovered.

Before our eyes the laity is finding its own dignity, even while the theologians discover new resources in St Paul and St John and their authentic gnosis. The laity, too, draws more freely on these sources, without any distinction of *pneumatici* or *psychici*. There is no aristocracy in the Church other than that of the saints, who often come from among men of small learning. And so, perhaps for the first time, the study of gnostics is no longer like studying some monstrously deformed embryos floating in their jars, but offers spiritual progress. That study does not set knowledge in the place of faith. But by its light it allows us to deepen our faith.

Arianism

ARIANISM IS SEPARATION IN ALL ITS PURITY. FOR MANY years it grew, almost imperceptibly, unnoticed even by sharp-eyed observers.

The Protestant Reform, which almost from the start grew up outside the Church, did not threaten the unity of the Church as much as Arianism did. The Reformation was led by a friar, a priest, laymen and princes: it never affected the leaders of the Church. There were no patriarchs or archbishops or eminent theologians or a pope to humor Luther and Calvin. From the beginning the battle was out in the open, the newness of the Reformation openly proclaimed. The Reformation did not have the protection of any worldly power comparable to that of an Emperor of Rome. And it occurred after sixteen hundred years within a Church that was full-grown, established, self-assured, and firmly organized around the See of Rome.

Arianism, on the contrary, is the archetype, never again seen to the same degree, of an almost unnoticeable error, the very model of semblance and temptation. It was the subtlest and most plausible doubt cast upon the very essence of the faith in Jesus Christ: Luther and Calvin would agree to this, I believe, as would Harnack, Barth, and other Protestant theologians.

Historic organisms such as nations or civilizations at times go through a critical period which brings out their resources, their strength, and their essence, and at the same time also shows up their most dangerous weakness. France, for example, achieves her greatest self-understanding in periods of revolution, because it is in these periods that her historians ask the most searching and incisive questions. The structure of the Church, too, stands out most clearly in her times of crisis. And among all the crises of the Church, Arianism was the crisis *par excellence*. It filled a century. Newman has seen this clearly; his whole work has its starting point in his meditation on the causes of the Arian success.

Arianism could become so dangerous because in some respects

79

it had the full weight of probability on its side. At first glance, the Arian doctrine is in complete harmony with the generally prevailing views of the Church. Orthodox historians dealing with a heresy incline at times to project the future into the past and make it seem as though the history that was still to come was already contained in the history that had gone before, as though the 'heretics' were heretics from the beginning, concealed like hidden traitors in the body of the Church. True history, however, must reach into the past to seize the diverse moments as they were when they were present, jutting out into the ocean of the unknown future like promontories.

If we are to understand the sources of Arianism, and its appeal, we must go back to its antecedents. I shall try to imagine the divine mystery such as the Gospel set it before the pagans and the Jews; and I shall try to state why, for vastly different reasons, it was unacceptable to either.

The Jews could not conceive how the divinity of the Messiah could be reconciled with the oneness of God, with the Divine Transcendence which they alone confessed in a world of idolaters. The faith of their fathers, purified and sharpened by the prophets, kept the presence of the One God constantly before them.

For the pagans, it was the other way around. They could readily understand that Jesus was a divine being, and were prepared to admit him into the company of their numerous gods. They were familiar with the notion that gods appear in human shape. There was no lack of heroes who had become gods, and of late there had been those emperors that had been deified.

But in one case as in the other, an infinite distance stretched between the Messiah and God, or between a god and God, and this distance grew only more unbridgeable as one tried to reduce it. If we draw a hexagon inside a circle and then increase the number of its sides, the difference between it and the circle grows constantly more noticeable. Just so, a Messiah and especially a Messiah conceived as the blessed son—in the official Jewish formulation, the beloved son—of the Father must in a radically monotheistic thought system remain a being infinitely different in substance from the infinite and single God alone in his transcendence, ineffable and unimaginable, whose only sanctuary was the Holy of Holies, the empty and symbolic room hidden within the one and only temple. To the Greek thinkers, however, who accepted the belief in Christ by conceiving of him as a mediator, the 'Son of God' Messiah was separate from that inaccessible God above all being whom great Greek philosophers like Plato and Plotinus had seen in glimpses.

In turn, Jews and pagans alike understood the existence of a mediator between the transcendent One and the world of men's minds. The Jews were well familiar with the idea of the mediating Word or Wisdom—the Word which is pronounced, the Wisdom which is created—whereby the Father communicated Himself to man and took possession of him. The pagan thinkers, too, had the idea of a mediating Intelligence or even Word, a first emanation of the first principle which reduced the distance between God and world. There were conciliators who thought that the Jewish concept of the Wisdom-Word and the Greek idea of the Intelligence-Word could be brought closer to each other. This idea can be found in Philo, a Hellenic Jew and contemporary of Christ who taught at Alexandria.

When Christ appeared in the flesh and in history, the task of the thinkers, after their first surprise, had been to understand him. To an intelligence embodied in a moment of time, to understand can only mean to apply existing thought systems to a new being. It was difficult to deny that Jesus of Nazareth was as human as any man. He had been born, he was dead, he had suffered. He had shared in man's life and man's condition, in all things like to us, sin excepted. Jesus had had God's power at his command, most of all in his resurrection. Explicitly and implicitly, he had spoken and acted as the sole and only-begotten Son, God's equal. In the extreme, he was one with God—in the utmost extreme, God like God yet without a breach in God's oneness. This was the faith that the first Christians had lived. Pliny, the Emperor's magistrate who observed them in their Sunday liturgy, wrote to the Emperor: 'They sing to Christ as to a god.' They worship. The depth of their faith remains inexplicable unless one accepts that Jesus Christ, Son of God, their Savior, is taken to be God himself, in the strict sense of the word God.

But as soon as the mind tries to understand there is no end of difficulties. Are we to think, after the manner of the mythologists, that God appeared in the shape of Jesus of Nazareth as though

Jesus were His symbol? Or that Jesus was a man who was united to God in a particular way and adopted by Him, made one with Him, like a privileged Saint among saints? Or that Jesus had been a passing historical act of God in the course and purpose of the history of salvation, so that his birth was one, or coincided, with his generation as God's only Son? It will be said that the texts of Scripture, especially St Paul's Epistles and even more the Gospel of St John, settled the question in favor of Jesus's divinity. But can we be sure? Had Scripture made the imprescriptible statement *Jesus is God* in the absolute sense? An exegete could hold with a great deal of plausibility that Scripture had done no such thing. The Old Testament, speaking of Wisdom, had stated plainly that Wisdom was created by God. The synoptic gospels put into Jesus's mouth affirmations of his humanity that seem to exclude his divinity. The Acts of the Apostles spoke of him as 'a man approved of God'. As to St Paul, all passages in which he spoke of Christ could be read to mean that Jesus was the most perfect of all creatures, the creature in whom all others had been willed, thought, predestined, and saved—but that he was not identical with God the Father.

The early Church Fathers had been perplexed by the distinction of the two births of the Word, one the eternal birth before all time of which St John spoke in the prologue to his gospel, the other the birth in time of Jesus of Nazareth born of the Virgin Mary which was written into the oldest expression of the faith. Certain others had let it be understood that the Word, Son of God, had had his beginning at the moment when he had entered history. It was difficult to make the distinction between the eternal Son of God, and the Son of God made man, especially so since the gospel is not a theology of the Divine Relations but a history of the relation of those Relations with man—a history of our salvation. The preaching of the Apostles and the teaching of Jesus take place on that concrete level of events which is in history. The Word that is speaking here is not the Word-as-such but the Word-Incarnate, son of the Virgin Mary. These difficulties are perennial. We need only to read the recent work of Professor Cullmann to realize that even some of our best informed scholars hesitate to state flatly that Jesus in the New Testament is a man who is one with God. Jesus, they specify, is God only insofar as

God reveals Himself in him. The divinity proceeds from his function rather than his being.[1]

To what extent had the Son existed before the Incarnation? To what extent is the Incarnation eternal?

With Athens on the decline, Alexandria was then the intellectual capital of the world, the city to which luminaries such as Clement, Origen, and Plotinus had lent lustre. It was even then the meeting place of East and West. It held the same fascination which later would prompt Leibniz to urge Louis XIV that he should unite the world from there, as Napoleon and Rommel did in fact attempt. It was the city where every synthesis was possible, the Gordian Knot of the worlds. And those were days when a synthesis of the minds of East and West was being sought. Plotinus had tried to combine Greek spirit with Indian inspiration, as Philo in Christ's time had tried to combine Greek spirit with Jewish revelation. Origen had mapped out a theology that was to be at once cosmic and Christian.

Arius was an ascetic rather than a mystic, an intellectual rather than a theologian. He could inspire rather than lead or guide. He was more passionate than ardent, more tenacious than strong, and more subtle than profound. In short, he was a reformer rather than a founder. As I try to see him at his best, unsullied by calumny or even criticism, I would say that his task was to make Christianity more accessible, to rid it of all cloudiness and especially of that oriental mysticism he had seen growing up in Alexandria. These he judged unacceptable both to minds tempered by Hellenistic culture, and to the laboring masses of the city's waterfront. He conceived God as simple, one, eternal, sublime, and infinite; and next to God, as close as possible but yet outside Him, was the reflection of His power and the most perfect of created beings: the Word, the *Logos* of St John. It remained true, of course, that *for us* the Word was like God, and could pass for God and be like Him. But *in itself* the Word was not God because He had been born, in short because there had been a time when He did not exist.

The success that this doctrine enjoyed in Alexandria with people of every kind is astounding. Among Arius' followers were

[1]Oscar Cullmann, *Christology of the New Testament*, 1959, Westminster.

ascetics and rigorists, impressed no doubt by his emaciation, his gravity, his self-mortification, and most of all his loyalty to Lucian of Antioch, who had died a martyr's death in 312. There were Egyptian women, attracted by this lean and lyrical personage who set all things in order. There were the sailors and laborers of Alexandria's dockside who saw in him a friend of the workers and a man who made religion simple and taught it in a chant whose beat fell in with the rhythm of their chores. There were also certain bishops, strangers to the allegorical and philosophical thought of the Egyptian schools. These were men who had held to the more humanistic and more exegetical or, as we would say today, more rational and more critical tradition of Antioch, Alexandria's closest rival.

Would it have been better to let the controversy wear itself out, to leave the rival schools of thought to live on as matters of opinion within the Church, as there had been opinions before Arius since the beginning? Such indifference would have been conceivable in a time of persecution, or in the days when the Church was underground and of no concern to the powerful. But in the meantime the most unlikely of all events had happened, with consequences that are felt to this day. The pagan Emperor had become a Christian. And not only that. Christianity, which until then had been outlawed, which to confess had meant death, had become the official state religion. Suddenly the impossible had become a fact. And Constantine, the Christian Emperor, was not at all reluctant to act as the pontifical peacemaker. He did so in the most natural manner in the world. He summoned the bishops of the Empire, East and West, to a meeting in Nicaea, near Constantinople. There the ancient formula of the faith was equipped with a supplementary definition. That definition condemned Arius' doctrine.

The new formula had been adopted with the consent of practically all the bishops. The crisis seemed ended. In fact it was beginning. That fact deserves a comment.

Had orthodoxy triumphed *too much*, perhaps at least in its formulations? In order to define the ancient faith, orthodoxy had introduced a new word, *homoousios*, consubstantial, which did not occur in Scripture. In the East that word had an unpleasant reputation. In 268, a local council of eighty bishops had rejected precisely this *homoousios*, when it condemned Paul of Samosata who had asserted that Christ was merely a man inhabited by an attribute of God. If the word meant 'of the same substance as' or 'identical with', it obviously rejected the distinction between the Son and the Father. It made of Jesus a manifestation of God, in keeping with the persistent idea of European rationalism as we find it, for instance, in Renan. The Fathers who in 268 condemned the word 'consubstantial' had made of it, for the East, the hallmark of the confusion of the Father with the Son. Rome did not know this, or did not care. In Rome, the word 'consubstantial' did not mean 'identical' but 'of the same essence'—God of God. Was it perhaps unwise to impose on the Asian Fathers such a change of meaning? The bishops in Nicaea had passed over that objection because the word disposed of Arius' error neatly and with precision. In doing so it explained the faith. And we may wonder with Karl Barth whether, with all its shortcomings inherent in all human speech, that word is not after all the one that expresses best what it wants to say. Words such as 'co-eternal', 'equal', or 'one with' could have been accepted by the Arians. The word 'consubstantial' could not, because to them it was Sabellian, modalist, implying confusion, and thus heretical.

Arius still had many sympathizers. The history of Arianism is among the strangest the Church has known. Before long the Nicaean Council was put in doubt, and the opponents of Nicaea came close to carrying the day.

Arius, a man of great self-assurance and skill, had powerful protectors at the Imperial court. Among them was the most cultured man by far of his day, a man of letters rather than a theologian, indifferent to right or wrong, lacking in firmness and largeness of mind, friend of the Imperial power, the resonant and subtle echo of his period: Eusebius of Caesarea, who may be called the father of ecclesiastical history. Eusebius knew everything: exegesis, geography, mathematics, and the rhetoric of the set speech. And Eusebius had a feeling that Nicaea had been a hasty victory, carried by surprise.

One of the theologians of Nicaea, Eustathius of Antioch, was a man who could not control his tongue. He liked to remind the world that the Emperor's mother had been an innkeeper's daughter. Constantine banished Eustathius to Thrace, and the See of Antioch fell to a friend of Arius. There followed a number of those changes of office-holders that have such great political importance. Arius caused his enemies to be removed. He was restored into the Church. He was preparing for a complete triumph when he died suddenly (336) in Constantinople. Constantine died the following year, baptized on his death-bed. In 350 Constantius, one of Constantine's sons who had long favored Arius, became sole Emperor. Constantius followed the advice of Eusebius of Nicomedia and of Eudoxus of Constantinople, who wished to make Arianism the official doctrine, just as Nicene Catholicism had been Constantine's doctrine. They would use the same methods as Constantine had used, convene ecumenical councils, and hammer out formulations of the faith.

It was, of course, impossible to proceed directly against Nicaea and its term 'consubstantial'. But one could relieve the partisans of Nicaea of their episcopal sees. Athanasius, bishop of Alexandria and champion of Nicaea, was exiled. Meetings of the bishops took place at Sardica and at Sirmium to work out confessions of faith in which the word 'consubstantial' was either omitted or else replaced by words akin to those of Nicaea but still acceptable to the opponents of the Nicene Creed. The Church resembled a parliament in session. None of the three formulas proposed at Sirmium contains the term 'consubstantial'. Some wanted to add an *iota* to the word *homoousios*, consubstantial, making it '*homoiousios*', 'of *similar* substance'. That little *iota*, under the guise of an insignificant correction, obviously destroyed everything that the Fathers of Nicaea had meant to protect against Arius' attack. The case strikingly shows the value of precision and the, at times, tremendous importance of a trifle.

Violence came to the aid of subtlety. Under the pressure of the powers, irregular meetings took place in the East. In 359 a 'Council' at Rimini in Italy attended by four hundred Western bishops, and another at Seleucia in Asia Minor with one hundred and fifty Eastern bishops, rejected the term 'consubstantial'. This was the moment of which St Jerome has written: *Ingemuit totus orbis et arianum se esse miratus est. (Adv. Lucif. 19).* The great episcopal sees were held by semi-Arians: Lisbon, Arles, Ravenna, and Sirmium in the West, Alexandria, Jerusalem, Caesarea,

Antioch, Nicomedia, and Constantinople in the East. In Rome, Pope Liberius had been banished. While working for a reconciliation he thought it wise to yield in a matter of personalities. He sacrificed Athanasius, the leading champion of the Nicene formulation.

For the moment itappeared that the Church would become semi-Arian and anti-Nicene, and would by implication condemn the legates of the Pope of Rome who at Nicaea had proposed the term 'consubstantial'. To all appearances the Church *was* Arian. We note in passing that the much greater terror of the persecutions in the early days had not been able to impair the faith.

But the faith of Nicaea, though silenced, was not dead. Athanasius played a leading rôle: one clear head is enough. He was a whole Church by himself, as certain generals are worth an army. The people recognized him as 'a good Christian and a true bishop'. His mind was clear and could clear other minds. His character was like steel. He was impervious to threats, subtleties, tricks or compromise. He drew fresh strength from every obstacle. He never yielded. In the teeth of the seeming success of the powers and of seemingly unanimous false decisions, in the teeth of the seeming 'dialectic of history' he stood up to defend 'pure quality', the truth. By his intelligent loyalty to the past he shaped the future. His voice was clear and steady and never dismayed, though he was condemned again and again by pseudo-councils. Supporting Athanasius and Hilary who controlled and briefed the clergy of Gaul, most of the laity had remained faithful. So had the Papacy, despite the prudent silence of Pope Liberius. Toward the end of the century Arianism lost ground and seemed defeated, only to reappear for a third time.

This second re-birth is one of the most extraordinary episodes in the whole history of the event. De Plinval has called it with good reason one of the extremely rare examples of the metempsychosis of an ideology. Arianism reappeared among those whom the Romans called the barbarians.

Arianism had penetrated into the provinces of the Danube. When the Goths occupied those provinces, they thus adopted the Arian form of Christianity. This was because Arianism much more than orthodoxy lent itself to those summary forms of faith that suit unpolished people. Its liturgy was secret, in the Gothic language, and took place during the night or at dawn. Its theology was crude and undeveloped. There were no monks. The affirmations of faith were violent, the piety had a military cast, and the Trinity had been all but cut apart. In short, it was a religion well adapted to peoples that had just emerged from Germanic paganism.

But these barbarians were then the dynamic element of European history. They were the Goths, the Ostrogoths, the Vandals, the Suevi, the Burgundians, the Rugians, the Alans, the Alemanni, and the Lombards. In the sixth century the new forces, the army, the young dynasties, the rising powers and the powers in possession were all Arian. Catholicism seemed outworn and defeated. And thus the situation remained until a most improbable event occurred: the rise of Clovis, a still un-Christianized barbarian and conqueror of the most powerful Arian state (507).

Clovis had a foreboding of the deep trend of history and felt the weakness of those who seemed powerful. He put his fighting force at the service of the Church, the bishops, and the monks of Nicaea. So the second wave of Arianism was conquered in its turn. The first wave had subsided even though it had had the support of the Empire and of cunning. The second, supported by the armies and kingdoms of the barbarians and by brutality, now disappeared from history.

What may seem surprising in this story is that the Church should have been so vulnerable in what mattered most, its faith. Newman expressed his astonishment that eminent bishops did not see what was at stake even though the faithful sensed it. And he concluded that the laity must not be neglected even 'in matters of doctrine'. Despite the excessive caution of Pope Liberius, the Nicene faith was saved by the convergence of the faith of the people with that of a few clear-headed and courageous bishops. It was saved against power and the friends of power, against the clever, the cunning, and the submissive. The like of it has not been seen again on the same scale—though it is not perhaps ruled out of the future of the Church.

The feat of Athanasius is astounding. Clear-headed, intuitive, and indomitable, he looms across the distance of history like another Abraham, the man in whom the future resided, and who stood alone.

In Arius' own thought, or at least in those tendencies of Antioch which inspired first him and later orthodox Fathers such as Theodoret, there may have been ideas that now were compromised by the obstinate resistance and that yet were valid. If so, they now had to go underground because of their accidental association with defeated Arianism. Every condemnation affects ideas and practices which in themselves may be prophetic but have become compromised by their association with condemned ideas. Among those who condemn another man, there are always some who condemn him for the falsehoods he has spoken, and some who condemn him for the truths he has offered. The truths are dragged along by the error at the core, as neutrons are dragged along by the atomic nucleus. Then the Church must agonize to recover her own. I mentioned this phenomenon when I discussed Montanism. We shall meet it again on a much larger scale in the Protestant Reform.

We turn to those elements in Arianism that foreshadowed the future.

Arius, as I said, had a lively feeling of the transcendence and inaccessibility of God. This feeling, which is strong again in our day, is one that has always animated both Christian and non-Christian mystics. It flows from conceiving God as above everything—even above being itself. 'He is more than being,' it is said, since 'being' still implies an analogy to the creature. Carried through to its conclusion such a doctrine would make God unthinkable; it would destroy the idea of Divine fatherhood, and the practice of prayer, including even the prayer of praise. But kept in balance, the idea of God's ineffable transcendence strengthens adoration. It keeps us from making of God a mere demiurge, an eternal fact, or an infinitely enlarged human being.

There was among the semi-Arian branches a very lively feeling also for the distinction between the Son and the Father. Joubert once said that the differences between Jansenists and Jesuits reside in this distinction. The Jesuits, he said, take from the Son to give to the Father; they respect nature and do not place redemption above everything else. The Jansenists take from the Father to give to the Son, and then have no means left to justify *nature, reason, creation,* or *essence*: everything is as if utterly annihilated in Jesus Christ.

Arius did, in fact, waver between these two tendencies. On the one hand he placed the Father above all else, and conceived the Son as being a super-creature. On the other hand he brought the Son closer to us and made him more human, more like us in substance. Whatever he may have said or asserted, the latter is the tendency that prevailed among his hearers and his faithful. There is good reason why Arius met such great response. Today we would say in Bultmann's language that Arius, by stressing the divine transcendence and its practically unknowable character, *demythologized* Jesus Christ. Like Renan and others of the 19th century, Arius doubtless imagined that he would bring Jesus closer to our emulation and to our hearts by stripping him of that mysterious 'divinity'.

What, then, was the most pressing task before the Church? First of all she had to safeguard the divinity of her founder against those who denied it and whom we might call the rationalists and humanists. Then, and only then, could she give a compensating emphasis to the humanity of Jesus. The theologians of the Reform sometimes suspected the average Catholics of being unconsciously monophysites who felt or even thought that Jesus was God and not a real man. In short, they suspected Catholics of not making a sufficient distinction between God and Jesus. The history of the Arian crisis may perhaps explain this tendency of the Catholic mind to see in Christ—for example in the Christ of the Eucharist—the Divine person rather than the human nature of 'the body and the blood'. During the long moment of the Arian crisis the reduction of Jesus to the status of a super-creature had been so strong that the Church cannot be blamed if she insisted with all her might on the Savior's divinity.

But we must still keep a balance, and preserve the structure of the truth. In our day the inclination of the modern mind, at least among critical exegetes, seems on the contrary to turn Jesus into a divine myth rather than a deified saint.

The mind of the Church of Antioch, which Arianism had threatened by emptying it of its essence, was nonetheless prophetic. Antioch insisted upon the historical element, called forth a literal study of Scripture, and brought Christ's humanity closer to our own.

Arius had made obstinate use of the passages in the Old and New Testaments that speak of a being in heaven 'in whom all things were made', and who would serve the Creator as a mediator to include within himself the whole history of the world. St Paul had applied the texts to Christ, especially in Colossians. This interpretation did, in fact, throw a retrospective light upon the Wisdom texts, and turned them into an announcement of the Incarnation; for that uncreated Wisdom was Jesus. But the Old Testament did not dare go so far, except in the Greek Book of Wisdom which comes close to teaching the divinity of the Wisdom. Still, the texts had something like two senses. One was the full sense, unheard-of and nearly impossible, in which they speak of a Being who is equivalent to God. The other was a lesser sense, more in keeping with the Greek mind and even with the monotheism of the prophets. In this second sense, the same texts could be speaking of a creature of the highest order, superior to all other creatures, intimately related to that uncreated Wisdom and yet different from it in that it was created. Arius had taken advantage of that ambivalence.

With the condemnation of Arianism the ambivalence was ruled out. The full sense of the texts was now distinct and clear: they refer to the eternal Christ eternally begotten. But the lesser sense was still there: it could call for the object to which it referred.

After Arius, a place remained open in the structure of heaven. Leverrier's computations had found a planet even before Galileo's telescopes pointed it out. In a like manner, the biblical texts pointed to a super-creature whom the telescopes had not yet found and named. It was the mother of Christ who, by analogy, would fill the void. The Wisdom texts which Arius had abused were in the liturgy quite naturally applied to Christ's mother. In this way, Newman suggested, Arianism prepared the intellectual structures that would help to develop Mariology. The neo-Arian theology of the Nestorians stood even now virtually condemned by the Council of Nicaea, and the road was open that would lead to the definition of the Virgin as 'Mother of God'.

In spite of all these strange and at times saddening turns of fortune that are painful to rehearse, in spite of the possibly contingent nature of the Nicene formulations, in spite of the injustices committed and of the wavering in the decisions, we may yet say that the formula of Nicaea saved the Christ-God, and therewith all religion.

Karl Barth is clearly aware of all this. His doctrine and his temperament both inspire him with an aversion to any theology imposed by the See of Rome. And yet he does not hesitate to state that the formulation *homoousios* by its usage, and by the clear meaning it received at Nicaea and still more after Nicaea, was definitively the only formulation which at that moment was capable, not of making the mystery comprehensible, but of keeping it from being dissolved.

The divinity of Christ, though it may find expression on the lips and in the cult of the faithful, will always be in danger. It is so great a *mysterium fidei*. It is almost impossible to understand that God is man in a true, real, and profound sense, and that Jesus is truly not a god, nor a superman, nor a super-god, in the sense in which there are multiple gods, but God Blessed in all eternity. Even St Paul himself possibly never dared to give explicit expression to the identity of Jesus with God. The clearest statement of the mystery is perhaps that in St John's gospel, despite the humble attitude of the incarnate Son before his sovereign Father. But then Nicaea brought the adamantine *consubstantialis*, balanced by the distinction between Son and Father and all the prepositions of the distinction: God *of* God, Light *of* Light. After that it was clear that Jesus was God in his profoundest essence, in his very selfhood. A clear formulation allows us to regroup elements that until then were scattered, a solemn oath clears the atmosphere. Just so the very form of the *definition* allows theology and faith to take a stride ahead and to deepen at the same time.

From now on it was no longer possible to remain in the Church while believing that Jesus was God only in a symbolic and mythical sense, *up to a point* or *at most*; or that he was Man-as-such, or the most wonderful of the children of men, or the greatest of mystics. Jesus was God, as he was God-of-God. His identity with God he received from God. Pragmatically, our attitude toward him had to be the same as our attitude toward God—there was no difference. The Eucharist may be adored.

What had from the beginning been the rule of the eucharistic action was henceforth firmly grounded in this mystery of identity in distinction, which is the most profound metaphysical revelation that we have about the Being *qua* Being. 'All is one, the one is in the other,' said Pascal.

The positive element in the heresy, which Arius had seen, understood, and foreboded, at the same time assumed its true place and was justified. The paradox and the privilege of condemnation consists, one might say, in that it saves the truth contained in the negative innovation despite the innovator. The condemnation of Arius made a true philosophy of mediation possible. Arius, I said, by means of biblical and patristic passages had staked out a type of existence within the universe of the mystery, that of the intermediary being. Until the scalpel had been used in the area of mediation to make a radical separation between the finite and the infinite, a source of ambivalence would remain and take its toll of the philosophers of mediation from Philo to Spinoza.

The fact that the Mediator is not somewhere in between, that he is not merely the most perfect of created beings but remains in his divine infinity, means that his mediation is sovereign because he does not cease being God even when he assumes human nature. He thus is Lord and Savior in all truth, not just by a dialectical process such as politicians or philosophers invent who create intermediate stages in an effort to fill the chasm between God and themselves. In the past such intermediate stages have been assigned to savior-gods, intelligible worlds, and Ideas; today there are the myths of the Fatherland or Evolution or Progress or the Proletariat or Humanity. The human intellect attempts to float a half-way station, a space satellite, upon the ocean of space between the Absolute and nothingness. But from now on this is out of the question. Any attempt to deify a part of man, of nature, or of the intellect in order to fill the abyss that separates nothingness from Being stands condemned as absurd from the outset because, in spite of certain appearances, it is historically incompatible with the foundations of Christianity.

After 325 it was thus no longer possible that certain attempts, then still in the distant future, could ever be made inside the Church: the attempt of German Romanticism or symbolic criticism to make Jesus into a near-God, a superman, or a symbol; nor even that attempt which would represent him as the terminal point of the Vital Force. The events of 325 instead made possible the Catholic thought system, which allows us to grant the highest dignity to the creature and yet to place between creature and Creator the infinite interval of adoration.

The events anticipated what was bound to happen to the religion of the Incarnation as soon as the Incarnation was put in question, as soon as a choice would once again have to be made between the pure mystery, and the mystery cut down, reduced to human proportions, and so fragmented. Renan, with his customary penetration, remarked that Arianism, 'which had the uncommon merit of converting the Germans before they came into the Empire, could have given to the world a form of Christianity susceptible of becoming rational'.

The humanly most probable course of events would have been the success of Arius, or someone like him, within a generalized semi-Arianism. It nearly happened, one might say, around the year 360. But in the event, what did happen was the improbable: a firm direction in Rome, the convergence of that direction with the general feeling of the faithful, the feat of Athanasius, the conversion to Christianity of Clovis—so many chance events that do not fit into what could then have been called the 'dialectic of history'.

The Arian movement did not, in fact, succeed in raising an Arian counter-Church against the Church. There was a pulling apart but no secession. It was the prototype of disjunction within an established and visible Church; while gnosticism had been the prototype of a crisis within a Church in process of formation. The former is perhaps a lesser threat to outward unity. Gnosticism fragmented thought and reduced the Church to a philosophy, or rather a whole bundle of philosophies and mythologies. Seen in this light, gnosticism called in response for the emergence of a strict definition of the data of revelation—that is, a directive theology. Marcion or Montanus were easily recognized; the case of Arius or of Eustathius was more difficult. The case of Pelagius was more difficult still, as we shall see. Here we are faced with the most secret crises that put the very principle of faith in jeopardy.

Arianism

I should add that Arianism, which began as a theological hypothesis and a plausible system, did in the end become established state doctrine, the leaven of the separated Church. Perhaps it was more liable than other doctrines to lead to Cæsaropapism, or at least to the confusion of the spiritual with the temporal. Reducing Christ to the proportions of a man, it was in harmony with the hidden desires of worldly power. And it was easily put to use.

There are other crises to be considered. A crisis might come from outside, for instance by the armed attack of one empire upon another. As we look at the map of the Empire in the late fifth century such a possibility appears remote. If the Empire is to succumb it will be to the blows of the so-called 'barbarians'— but the barbarian kingdoms are Christian. The West has won out. And what ideas or what forces are there to fear from the East? Judaism has no strength left. Even when Israel was strong it did not sally forth to proselytize or to conquer. It waited for what came its way, and did not go out to meet others. Israel was not warlike.

The improbable happened, and our surprise has lasted to this day. A race appeared in history, a race not Jewish. A man appeared, an empire was formed, and all in a short time. Only the rapid extension of Slavic communism bears comparison with that surging rise, that conquest, and those extreme dangers.

95

Islam

Understand me, and kill me. (Arab proverb)

WHEN THE ARIAN CRISIS WAS OVER, IT LOOKED AS though the Church might for a while have peace. In fact, she was to suffer an attack from the outside, perhaps the gravest attack ever made on her, and one that is not yet over.

The paganism of the Romans, the Germans, the Slavs, and the Mongols had been unable to break the Church. Christianity, it seemed, had triumphed once and for all over the enemy outside. Armies watched even over the Church of Nicaea. The garrisons of Italy, once Arian, were orthodox. There seemed to be no quarter from which resistance, let alone an invasion, could come; no organized enemy was anywhere in sight. The only possible enemy the Church might have left would have to be within herself: in her own decadence.

But what happened, in fact, was that the Roman-Christian world was all but destroyed by nomadic desert tribes, caravans without armies, without culture and almost without an existence, armed only with one single absolute weapon: their faith in that single God who was also the God of the Christians and the Jews.

Within a few years of their first assault, Syria fell to them, the center of the faith; then Egypt with Alexandria, capital of learning; and the Mediterranean, that 'Catholic lake'. In the life span of one man, half of the territories and resources of the Roman Empire was in Mohammed's hands. A hundred years after his death, Mohammed's troops stood at Poitiers in the heart of France, and had reached India, the Eastern counterpart of Alexandrian Egypt.

It is noteworthy that the population in their path who until then had been Christians accepted the doctrines that Mohammed had preached. One does not commonly think of him as a 'heretic'. His doctrine, thought, and religion had developed outside of the Church, while 'heretic' usually means a man whom the Church has cast out. However, I shall not tarry here over their classifications, but consider Islam as if it were a vast division split off from Christianity.

Christianity, like all religious revolutions, is in a sense an attempt to achieve greater consistence and purity. Jesus simplifies and elevates Moses. Christianity, simpler in its practices and code of duties, and altogether centered on the mysterious person of Jesus Christ, has a more universal range than Judaism with its overload of ritual. The very success of Christianity shows that it answered to the unconscious aspirations of the masses, who often need a simpler religion than is commonly offered to them. But the spread of Christianity was limited by the exalted nature of its dogma, and by the demands of its morality which called on man to renounce himself, to overcome his selfishness, and to love even more than adore.

After six centuries of success and opposition one might almost have predicted what sort of religion would achieve the greatest immediate success in a civilization that was still steeped in paganism, and was now occupied and inhabited by a Christianity which, though growing, was still poorly assimilated. The new religion would have to be still simpler, simple after a rather primitive and elementary fashion in its beliefs and practices, and offering greater concessions to human nature than either Judaism or even more Christianity had been willing to make.

One could imagine a certain mixture combining all the most attractive features of mysticism with all that is most seductive in the complete triumph and freedom of the flesh. If ever a mixture could be found that would combine the mystic and the carnal spirit, if an amalgam of these two extremes were possible, if nature could ever be made whole and without injury, we would certainly be face to face with a very powerful religion.

To put it differently: If there should arise a simplifier capable of carrying away the masses and captivating the multitudes, a man who could draw from Christianity its essence, adapt Christian morality to the instincts of the crowd, dispel the anguish of predestination by unmistakable signs, and point a sure way to success both in this world and in eternity—in short, a man who could offer religion as a technique of salvation even while following one's instincts, he would have a religion that would triumph, and triumph quickly.

Islam

529 79

Arianism, one might say, was in part such a religion. Arius had simplified not so much the dogma as the manner in which the Christian conscience imagined Jesus Christ. Arius had taken the idea of Jesus down a step to bring it closer to the pagan mind. He had already pronounced the fatal word 'only'. To him, the Father was the *only* God, the *only* Holy One, the *only* Highest. We can still read it in the *Gloria*, if indeed the *Gloria* is an Arian hymn corrected and adapted to Christ, as Duchesne thought: *Tu Solus Sanctus, Tu Solus Dominus* . . . Calvin, too, would later insist on the *only* faith, the *only* God. Every time we pronounce the word 'monos' or 'solus' or 'only', we simplify. By the exclusion of moderation, we leave no room for doubt and anxiety. An absolutist doctrine is at first invigorating, since it relieves us of the claims of prudence and proportion which cause the anguish of uncertainty.

The Arabia from which Islam has come was not a desert in those days. There was a happy Arabia nestling along the trails of the oases which supported a vast reservoir of men. These men possessed the art of irrigation, and knew the uses of metal and of horse and camel. The fetishist and animist religions of the Arab world before Mohammed tended to join forces in a sort of monolatry at Mecca, center of trade and pilgrimages, with its magic cube that held the Black Stone called the Ka'ba, God-symbol of the Quraish. Arabia was neither a void not a wasteland, but a place where the images, ideas, and motifs of primitive Judeo-Christianity with its apocalyptic forebodings, handed on by Christian, Nestorian or Jacobite preachers, took a new lease on life. From the Judeo-Christians with whom he came in contact Mohammed had heard of the ancient prophets of Israel, and learned something of the doctrine of Jesus and the apostles. This Judeo-Christianity, desiccated and submerged, as I have mentioned, was in a way destined to be the soil on which the Koran would thrive. The Koran took up Judeo-Christianity in several points, to fill it with the tender and enchanting poetry of the Arabs and the simplifying fire of the desert. Mohammed believed that Abraham had come to Mecca, there to rebuild the Ka'ba with the help of his son Ishmael.

Mohammed, a poor orphan of the tribe of Hashim, had

101

married the rich widow Khadija, and from their marriage had come the tender and gentle Fatima. Fatima, by her marriage with Ali, would in time give birth to countless descendants of Mohammed. Toward his fortieth year Mohammed, disgusted with fetish worship, embraced the idea of a single God. As a young man, soft-eyed and black-haired, he had begun to prepare himself for a larger world. His mind was troubled with a deep unrest that is shown in his wavering between the extremes of his nature. At times he was ferocious to the point of cruelty, or cunning; at other times smitten with God, fearful of Judgment, generous and gentle. Gaudefroy-Demombynes says that Mohammed had the virtues and the vices of our own age. He points out also that if Mohammed had not been above all else a mystic he would not have been able to overcome his inner conflicts.

This troubled and violent dreamer, whose mind had matured to the swaying rhythm of the long, slow caravans, was seized by an ecstatic trance, as sorcerers were seized by djinns. He believed what he heard within himself. Like the soothsayers of ancient Arabia or the Hebrew Nabhi, or like the first Christian mystics who spoke or heard 'unknown languages', or again like a surrealist poet or a Victor Hugo conjuring up spirits on the Isle of Guernsey, so Mohammed received a revelation which he was bold and artless enough to record just as it came to him. Allah speaks to him through Gabriel seated on a cushion of brocade and silk. Mohammed snorts like a young camel. The angel shows him a cloth on which the revelation is written. The angel reads it to him. Mohammed recites it. And so the *book*, unlike the book of the Jews which was composed over long centuries by prophets and the priesthood, was here received as if it fell from the sky in the absolute moment of the desert.

This was not the long and slow and many-voiced experience of a people, as is the Bible of the Jews, nor the public announcement of the Messenger, as is the Gospel. What Mohammed entrusted to writing was the poem of a soul, or rather the psychoanalytic transcript of the personal inspiration of an unconscious mind, a welter of mystical and dogmatic views, political rules, words of wisdom and moral counsel, confidences about his love life, calls to holy war, and visions of the end of time, hell, and paradise. And Mohammed, the Poet supreme who has faith in everything that comes from within him, passes this faith on to his people. The psalmody of the Koran, put together haphazardly, becomes the sole sacrament of this people. It was not a book, but Mallarmé's book-as-such, the prototype and Great Mother of the book.

Having taken dictation from the angel, Mohammed dictated in turn. His words were taken down on the spot, on palm bark, a sheep's shoulder-blade, or a flat stone. Twenty years after his death a text was edited, divided into one hundred and sixteen *suras* or chapters, with the longest placed at the beginning.

The religion which Mohammed preached was a prophetic monotheism, simplified and reduced to the bone. It started from nothing. Unlike Judaism, it had no prior tradition to preserve. Unlike the earliest Christianity there was no testimony about miracles that needed to be kept in order. Mohammed stood at the prow of time like a new Abraham—with no Messiah to wait for, no promise.

Subjection to the One God, and the belief that Mohammed is His prophet ruled out the two opposites that were then so much before men's eyes. It ruled out trinitarian Christianity with its adoration of Jesus, and it ruled out idolatrous paganism. Islam was the path along the mountain ridge between two chasms. The commandments are precise and clear, and need no commentary: You must pray, give to the poor, fast, and go on pilgrimage. Morality consisted in the help given to one's brothers of the same race. A friend had everything to hope, an enemy everything to fear. It will be said that this morality was accommodating. It is, of course, true that it accommodated the warlike spirit, and the violence of war—but not justice, hospitality, or the eventual freeing of the slaves. Nor did it make the union with God easier, because it left man's conscience all to itself, without a guide, without a mediator, without theological concepts—face to face with the one and infinite God.

At most it could be said that Islamic morality did not like Jewish morality focus on the idea of a permanent and direct relation between conscience and action, the idea of the sense of sin or responsibility. Socially, Islam meant liberation of the poor, the humble, the masses of small traders and little people, the slaves, the freedmen, and the hungry. Mohammed raised his voice against the abuses of the merchants and the rich. Out of the disinherited, he formed the future group of the predestined.

Mohammed was opposed by those in possession and those who favored the existing order. Some merchants of the town of Yathrib offered him asylum. He left Mecca on a day later said to have been July 16, 622. This is the *hegira*, or migration, the birthday of the Islamic era which is the only one of all the non-Christian eras that has clearly endured.

Successful beyond his fondest expectations, and with his mystique justified by a political triumph that exceeded his intentions, Mohammed lost himself in the bondage of sensuality. At the same time, his initial monotheism acquired a twin, mono-prophetism. This, now, is Mohammedanism. Decadence of this sort is a familiar spectacle; we have seen it in Victor Hugo. The strength of this religion, as I said, lay in that it never troubled about the world, or time, or space. There was one God and one prophet; no God-man, no divine-human mystery. Jesus had humbled himself before God, even while making himself equal to though not identical with God. Mohammed, on the contrary, never calls himself 'the Son of Allah' and never claims to be His equal; but he lets it be understood that he is the Only One. To call upon Mohammed's name comes to be necessary for salvation. He is the 'seal of the prophets', a new Solomon but without any consciousness of carnal sin. He has nine legitimate wives, beside concubine slaves. From now on his politics know no scruples. In order to unify the first and very mixed community, and also add to his resources, Mohammed made raids upon the infidels. He tied a white standard to the lance of Hamza, first leader of a band of thirty, and so lent a sacred character to these acts of brigandage in the Arab tradition.

The Muslim seem to have extolled not so much the blood shed by the martyr who bears witness, as the blood spilled by the fighter who conquers in the name of Allah. Beyond the sword lies paradise. Other religions preached holy wars only incidentally —the Muslim religion made it for long its central act. Up to the moment when Europe rallied and took certain great technical strides, the Muslim's holy war appeared as the supreme danger. To the force of their arms they added the force of fanaticism.

War was the sacral act; it took the place of the sacrifice. Death in battle meant salvation. Had Mohammed wanted holy war? Whether it was the result of his temperament and his race rather than of his faith, holy war became the catalyst of an Arab world that until then had been scattered, despised, and crushed by Greek culture, Roman rule, Jewish proselytism, and the Christian apostolate. The Christians were the enemy because they held the territories which the Arabs coveted. As Lenin's logical and hard doctrine became an instrument of pan-Slavism, and Calvin's doctrine was put to the service of Anglo-Saxon expansion, so Islam came to serve pan-Arabism.

The Arab faith, fanatical though it be, is also practical and of considerable organizing power. Light cavalry and an infantry of archers, and engines brought from Persia or copied from Byzantium, combined to form the best army of the times. From their place at the hinge of the two worlds, the horsemen of Allah spread to the West and to the East. What is astonishing is that these lightning conquests have had such lasting effects.

Jerusalem fell in 638, and ever since that day the Temple has been a mosque. In 643 the Arabs had reached the Caucasus, and the Indus. Carthage fell in 698. By the eleventh century the Christendom of Africa had disappeared, not to emerge again for eight hundred years.

There were in the Eastern territories many who preferred to surrender to Mohammed rather than bow to Byzantium. They were moved by a lively hatred for Constantinople, a preference for the worse, a quest of vengeance or of novelty, and also by a certain Muslim tolerance for the Christians, the 'men of the book'.

Fifty years after Mohammed's death his horsemen breathed the air of the Atlantic. Spain, suffering from the same sickness as Byzantium—the confusion of Church and State—succumbed quickly. In 711 Tarik the Moorish chief overcame King Roderic.

Paradoxically, Islam was at first more favorable to the advancement of science than was Christianity. The convert peoples of Africa and the East had shown an aptitude for language and rhetoric, but had not taken to philosophical or mathematical abstraction. Christianity had taken over the form rather than the substance of the Greek heritage. The elite of the peoples converted to Islam were less worldly than the Arabs, and more susceptible to beauty of form than to subtleties of thought. The Jewish and Christian sages, particularly those among them who had become hellenized, had not concerned themselves with defining the extremes, heaven and earth, the godhead and man; rather, they had applied themselves to defining the rules and concepts which are like the rungs of the ladder that leads from zero to infinity, and from the world of the senses to the world of God. For all these reasons the Graeco-Roman Christians, contemplative and systematizing, had not encouraged invention and technology and the technical labors of what is called science.

In this they remained faithful to an ancient distrust of technical progress. The earliest Jews had had a foreboding of the abuses to which sinful man would put the technical sciences, which are so quick to have abominable consequences. The story of Cain expresses that foreboding, the story of the Tower of Babel, and perhaps even the story of the forbidden fruit, symbol of utilitarian science.

It cannot be said that the bedouins of the Hejaz, strangers to all forms of civilization and carrying on by raid and by feud, had any special aptitude for technology. But those who start with nothing have the advantage of being unencumbered. Knowledge is always in danger of going around in circles, mistaking its own existence for its ultimate goal and so being of use only to philosophers, scholiasts, and mandarins. The Arabs did not avoid this danger: even the Koran supports its caste of explicators. But they had the practical turn of mind of the Semites, and their unparalleled success in battle gave them a confidence in their race without the inferiority feeling of the Jews: no one has ever seen a Muslim captured, persecuted, or enslaved! Their enemies watched the Arab expansion from their ramparts, and at times reconquered an Arab advance post. But until the nineteenth century they never held Arab lands for any length of time.

The world of Islam fell heir to Greek culture, and Arabic became the scholar's language in the West. The Arabs knew astronomy, medicine, trigonometry, geography, algebra and geometry. By a chain of events that still seems improbable to the imagination, the masterpieces of the Greeks came to be known in the West through Latin translations made from Arabic translations, after having twice donned the wrong garments, one too light, the other too heavy. This is how Aristotle reached the West, Aristotle who had done what Hegel had dreamed of doing, to write an encyclopedia of all human knowledge. And it was Aristotle who gave to the West what Karl Marx in our time has given to communism: that systematic and ordered knowledge which is so necessary for massive indoctrination.

The ways of God, said St Paul, are inscrutable. From where we stand, His detours are ironic.

Classical Greece, Christianity, and Islam crossed paths twice without mingling. The first time was in ninth century Baghdad, thanks to the Abbasid caliphs and their patronage of the arts. Christian influences were felt in Damascus, as they had been since the days of St John Damascene. In Medinah the three-termed Aristotelian syllogism replaced the two-termed logic of the Semites.

The second encounter took place at Toledo and Burgos in Spain, at Naples, and in Sicily. Stimulated by the Greek example, original thinkers such as Kindi, Farabi, Avicenna and Averroes arose among the Muslim, and such as Isaac Israeli, Ibn Gabirol, and Maimonides among the Jews. Without that Arab-Muslim culture, could the great scholastics have come to be? St Thomas takes issue with the Muslim thinkers who are for him what the 'gentiles' were to St Paul. He hopes to convert them by turning their own premises against them—a perennial principle of Christian dialectics, reflecting the idea that error is not so much a fault as an inconsistency, an unfaithfulness to one's own self.

One may wonder whether the melodic poems of the Muslim, with their rhymed refrains the *zajal* and the *muwashshah*, have not influenced the troubadours and the Catharists. For, after all, the two heirs to Greek culture on the Mediterranean, the Church and Islam, did not after their first clash isolate themselves from each other until the seventeenth century. They may well have met. There had been communities that combined Arabs with Christians, Jacobites, or Nestorians. But then supervened the laicization of the West, the torpor of the East, and the two cultures turned into something worse than enemy cultures: sealed vessels, without communication.

As we take the large view of this history of Islam and compare it with other cultures, we shall encounter two surprises.

One is the astounding speed of the devouring fire. We have seen it before: the rapidly growing pace, the frenzy, the collapse before it, the shameful feeling of relief among those who yield to fear, to weariness, or to the secret hope for a liberator, the charismatic appeal—*baraka*—of the conquerors combined with the misery of the conquered—all this we know. Recent examples are before our eyes. But those empires that grow out of all proportion are like the reptiles of the Jurassic. They soon dissolve, they do not last. We need only recall Alexander, Attila, Ghengis Khan, Charlemagne, Napoleon. Their history seems in the retelling like a passing illusion.

And then, the second surprise: Islam has lasted, and it is still lasting. According to statistics it now numbers three hundred million faithful. It is a considerable material and spiritual force. Besides, it further shows a remarkable material and spiritual impenetrability. During the Arab Conquests or in the age of the Crusades, there existed a certain equality of resources. The Arabs had the same weapons, the same navies. However, they did not join in the technical enterprise of the West. One would have thought that this was their own loss. What could they do against cannons, torpedoes, tanks, planes, rockets? They had to pay their tithe, of course, to a heavily armed West; they used cunning, subterfuge, and for a time they submitted. But in the end the desert, underground resistance, obstinacy, guile, self-sacrifice, and terror proved stronger than the armed force of the West.

And what are we to say of the relations of Islam with Judaism and Christianity, its two sister religions descended from Abraham like Islam itself?

There have been centers of an Arab-Christian and an Arab-Jewish culture. The law of the Koran even extended its protection to the 'people of the book'. In the beginning, Mohammed had sought a rapprochement with the Jews; he had the prayer facing toward Jerusalem, and had come each Saturday to lead the midday prayer in the mosque at Gaba. And there had been the so-called Constitution of the Year One, masterpiece of international politics. That union did not last. In 624, Mohammed proclaimed that the true believer must turn toward the *gibla* of the Ka'ba, toward Abraham. This meant the definitive isolation of the Muslim from Jews and Christians. The Jews and Christians remained as *dimmi*, paying the poll tax of the unbeliever, unless they were willing to interpret pentateuch and gospel by the Koran.

The Muslim have proved more impenetrable to the Christian mission and evangelization than the Jews. They are so far from considering Christianity superior to their own faith that they have at times even allowed the Church to expand, and to set up and operate her institutions, even schools, in their very midst. They sent their most gifted sons to these schools without a moment's fear that the Christian faith might win out. It is true, of course, that for a Muslim conversion to Christianity means to be stricken from the record, cast out completely; it means a loss of his civic status and national existence, besides his rejection by God. But the Muslim contempt for the idea of conversion to Christianity as even a possibility does not rest on these legal and civic defences. He has the unshakable conviction that he is superior to Jew and Christian alike. The conviction springs no doubt from his awareness of the hypocrisy of a West that does not practise what it preaches concerning prayer, for example, or worship, fasting, poverty, or social justice. The Muslim is shocked to witness how Christianity since the Middle Ages has allowed its social and national life to grow ever more secular, until many Christians live today like superstitious unbelievers rather than disciples of Jesus Christ. Indeed, educated and cultivated Europeans who have lost their faith in God at times find their way back to their catholicism merely by a contact with Islam.

There is a trifling number of exceptions, just large enough to show that the conversion from Mohammed to Christ is not impossible to uncommonly well-informed and courageous souls. But it has so far been so rare as to be practically non-existent. Missionaries who are yearning for Muslim souls have been compelled by this practical impossibility to abandon the gospel maxim *Euntes docete*, to give up any attempt at conversion by the word, and be content instead with silence, prayer, and their mere presence, in the manner of Father de Foucauld. There is one lonely glimmer in this black-out of encounter, the Benedictine monastery at Toumliline, the only mystic breach through which the Christian West and the mystic Islam may converse. Since the Muslim religion is a daily liturgy of worship, contact with Christianity can clearly take place only outside the Abbey. Does the same situation hold in India, and in China? Where preaching, the apostolate, and example fail, only spirituality remains—pure prayer in poverty. Perhaps it is around centers such as these that the spirits may regroup themselves some day.

One of the reasons for the success of Islam in Africa lies in its understanding of the Negroes. Long before the Europeans, Islam had colonized the Negroes as far as Mauritania and the Senegal. Yet Islam did not appear to be a colonizer. Islam made no concessions to the paganism that preceded it, nor did it claim to reveal to the Negroes the Rights of Man. It merely drew a few consequences from the Koran, which is like a simplified Old Testament, and respected the primitive traditions of the Negro countries. It did not have recourse to missionaries, at least not at the start. In anticipation of what Christianity has only just rediscovered, Islam intended that it should be spread by the Negroes themselves. Having itself emerged from animism, Islam was sensitive to the religious values in those elementary forms of the religious life which to the European seemed for long pure fetishism. It took the genius of Father Libermann, a converted Jew, to realize from 1850 onward that Negro animism ought to be developed, not destroyed.

What can account for this persistence of Islam through so many centuries, which gives Mohammed a posterity larger than that of Moses, and renders Islam insensitive to the blows or pleas of Christianity, whose doctrine is so much higher?

Renan, never one to avoid a problem, asked himself the same question. In his discussion of the Judeo-Christian attempts to simplify Christianity, he observes that 'if these attempts had suc-ceeded they would have prevented Mohammed's success among the Arabs and the Syrians'. According to him; 'Christianity is a version of Judaism adapted to the Indo-European taste; Islam, a version of Christianity adapted to the Arab taste.' Mohammed, Renan says, 'did after all only go back to the Judeo-Christianity of Zenobia, in reaction against the metaphysical polytheism of the Nicene Council and the Councils that followed'. In this remark Islam is joined to the discordant chorus of heresies. It would be a heresy by its refusal to grow and develop. And it is true that Mohammed retrenched and simplified: he made historic time stand still as Joshua did the sun.

But we must underline once more that to this simplification there was added a most powerful resource, the harmonization of contraries. Of all religions, the religion of Mohammed has more than any other united contradictions: blood, lust, death, the difficult and reassuring ritual, the worship of a sole and trans- cendent God—sensuality, frenzy, violence, cunning—and the most unencumbered and most constant spirituality, ceaseless prayer in a nature that is void. Islam is the form of religious life which identified itself most fully with the misery and the grandeur of a race until then despised, but unassailable as are all races because it always draws new life from its roots. War among races is a biological fact that threatens to re-emerge despite all Christian and lay attempts to give legal status to the equality of the human person, to man's solidarity regardless of differences in body structure or appearance. The color of the skin, seemingly so secondary, often separates as if it were a biological uniform that cannot be taken off.

It may be said that Mohammed drew strength from what he retained of Christianity and made more readily assimilable to untutored minds. He drew from it the ideas of the brotherhood of all believers, and of salvation assured by faith together with the apostolate and proselytism. That separation of laity and clergy, which cost Christianity some of its cohesion, did not exist in Islam. In principle the Mohammedan layman is a solitary levite who worships God as does the monk. In making all believers contemplatives, without imposing ascetic rules on their sexuality, Mohammed secured for his religion a great deal of prestige.

By his devil-may-care disregard, he solved this nagging question of right sexual practice which for the Christian, especially the Catholic, is the most difficult part of morality. Second, he solved the theological problem by voiding the mystery. One may say that, third, he solved the question that would be the sore point of every Western establishment: the social question, the problem of the rich and the poor. There was no longer slavery, because a slave who embraced Islam was on that instant free. Usury, the means of domination which cuts mankind in two, one free to move, the other tied by what cannot be untied, was forbidden. Mohammed, it could be said, spread hope of liberation, as did the French Revolution, and to this spirit he owed not so much his initial success as the endurance of that success.

Finally, Islam reconciled faith and reason. The most mystical faith was reassured each day by the renewal of prayer, each year by a long and difficult fast, each lifetime by a pilgrimage. On the other hand rationalism, that perennial temptation of the thinking species, was satisfied by the exclusion of every mystery except that of the single God, source of the urge to think. An Arab philosophy was born and grew as there had been a Jewish philosophy. But Islam no more than Israel has seen the birth, the growth, or the branching out of a theology.

At no time in its long career has Islam faced an encounter like that of today.

The problem is to know how the Arab world will bear up under the contact with the world around it against which it has so far been protected by distance, fragmentation, or its own contempt for it. The Arabs have been able to avoid all forms of rapprochement with Christian humanism and industrial technology, with this Christian and lay society where the Church is separate from the State and woman about to emancipate herself; so full of ambiguities in conduct, and in the variety of meaning it gives to such words as 'liberty', 'equality', or 'love'. True liberty and true equality—the Arab has seen them at home, under his own eyes, in the submission to the same God and the same Law. The secular West had taken a different road, and on that road the Christian faith of the prophets had let itself bog down.

Islam could guard itself against the practising atheism of the West only by opposing everything that came from the West: all contacts with the Occident were considered deadly. Christianity, which opposed the summary and cruel faith of Islam, was deadly. And deadly also was the anti-Christianism of the West, which, had it triumphed, would have forced Islam to stop worshipping God. This resistance in two directions compelled Islam to reject *en bloc* this ambiguous West which is both Christian and anti-Christian and blind to its internal contradiction. If Islam is as hostile to one as to the other, it is yet more hostile, and rightly so, to their mixture.

The strength of Islam was to negate time in order to conquer space, never to move, to grow rigid. But now it will have to adopt the technology, if nothing else, of the West, and with it certain features of the Christian heritage: the sense of man, of woman, of the universal. Will Islam be able to humanize, to 'feminize' itself, above all to become universal, and yet not have to face within itself the disappearance of that loyalty to race which is of its very essence, even more than Judaism? Can there be such a thing as a neo-Islam, analogous to Christianity, that neo-Judaism? Can there be a second Mohammed who would be to the Prophet as Jesus was to Moses? If so would it still be Islam?

The fetishist paganism from which Islam has risen and which it respects down to its Black Stone, was on its way toward the worship of the One. The same can surely not be said of atheist Marxism. Since 1917, year of the new hegira, atheist Marxism is taking shape under our eyes, by a process not unlike that of Islam at the time of Mohammed. The analogy has struck some profound students. Again we see the attempt to combine a simplifying and mystic doctrine that promises salvation within the reach of all, with the expansion of a people, an army, and a party. Its successes are so rapid and so vast that one can barely follow them—we would rather close our eyes. Entire walls of the ancient world are tumbling. The West vacillates between appeasement and resistance, in the name of certain human and Christian values summed up in the ancient word *Liberty*.

The two Islams—how will they act one on the other? What will the meeting of Mohammed and Lenin be like?

In the African countries Islam and communism encounter a common enemy, the white man from Europe. Islam has fought Christianity actively for a thousand years. Its virulence is unabated, and its power may revive at any moment. The armed force of Islam has declined since it stood under the walls of Vienna, but the number and the conviction of its adherents has not. Although Islam has lost regions where it ruled over Christian majorities, it has won new followers in Asia and especially Africa.

Islam controls the junction between East and West, and surrounds the ancient centers from which Christian religion has spread out—and which are now oil-well country.

One might ask whether Islam might not on the contrary be the strongest barrier to a Marxist invasion of Africa, or whether the East might not be likely to set an example to the West, even the Christian West, of the purest values in their elementary and sparsest form. Arab spirituality has often been of help in just this way to Westerners who had lost themselves in technical success, search for efficiency, or Western secularism. That great uniting cry of the muezzin resounding over the towns of the East has led certain Christians, including Psichari and de Foucauld, back to the source. In Spain, too, the contact between Christian and Muslim spirituality has suggested techniques of self-divestment to some mystics.

As we pursue this hopeful line of thought, we may ask further whether Islam might not become the area of mutual understanding between Judaism and Christianity. To do so, Islam would have to shake off its spirit of exclusiveness, its narrowness, and its hatred of Christianity. That spirit is rare, no doubt, among the elite and the masses, who have stayed healthy and hospitable and have preserved their treasure of kindness and openness. It survives mainly in that third part which consists of the bourgeoisie, the intellectuals, and the politicians.

Dare we hope that the Muslim community might some day cross the line of race, and undertake the mission to bear witness to God against all idols?

The Jews, though held together by race, have escaped from the enclosure of the common blood. They did it by dispersion, by their fusion with various European nations, at times by secularizing their faith into a purely temporal messianism of progress, and by the part they played in the revolutions of the West. They have upheld Abraham's vocation, his universal openness whose symbol is the starry heaven with its multitudes.

Louis Massignon said more than once that in this world the Jews represent Hope, the Muslims Faith, while Love falls to the lot of the Christians.

So far, the Muslims have not opened out into the universal. They remain the living witness of what the Jewish warriors might have done but failed to do—they established a victorious military theocracy on a vast racial scale. And yet there comes the moment when Islam hears the call of the Universal, understood in terms of peace. Can one derive a universal doctrine from the Koran? Can one find in it a common foundation of monotheism acceptable to all, that stands up to an atheism militant and triumphant? The spiritual strength of Islam, despite the many weaknesses due to that very strength, is that it bears witness to the God of Abraham—that it can chant the first words of the Nicene formula, *Credo in unum Deum* . . .

Cardinal Nicholas of Cusa thought that neither Christ nor even Moses could have impressed himself at first encounter upon the barbarian populations of Arabia, and that an intermediate stage was therefore necessary. The Cardinal of Cusa asked himself if Islam was not this intermediate stage. He wondered whether it was really desirable that Islam should be converted to Christianity too soon; whether a long preparatory phase was not needed—in the manner of those teachers today who are content to be a living presence of Christianity amid the Arab people, and do not attempt to convert the Muslim élite. Father de Foucauld showed to the Muslim an example of a contemplative life lived in poverty. The idea here is that conversion is the work of God, and demands a patience equal to the patience of the God who allowed so many empty centuries from Fall to Incarnation.

Fundamentally, Mohammed's principal inspirations were drawn from the catholic world in those countries which the Romans had never bothered to conquer and civilize. Mohammed, it has been said, preached to unpolished and idolatrous pagans a Christian religion reduced to extreme simplicity. For example, he preached the doctrine of the absolute oneness and radical omnipresence of God which was the basis of original Judaism; he preached the religion of kindness and equality, the doctrine of creation, and the doctrine of angels, good and evil spirits; he preached the doctrine of punishment and eternal reward.

Jesus was not denied—He had his place among the prophets. Mohammed, it has been pointed out, would have accepted the Jewish idea that mankind would be judged by Christ; it was not he, Mohammed, but Jesus who would judge mankind. The mother of Jesus, Our Lady Mary, was to him first among women, model of womanhood. Mohammed's disciples had retained from the first apostolic Fathers a vague idea of what would later be called the 'Immaculate Conception'. The Jews who slander Mary are treated harshly, and are called infidels because

> They did not believe in Jesus,
> They invented against his mother an atrocious lie.
>
> (*Koran*, 4, 155)

The yellow race will take the place of the white race. If indeed communism is to find in China its most radical application, and there impose a type of mystico-technological civilization which is Russian only in origin, then the civilization of the future will find its expression in the expansion of the yellow race. Islam, now, has greater affinities with the yellow race than have the whites, for it is an oriental phenomenon, while the Slavs are still the last 'barbarians' of the occident. The orient will resume the leadership on the day when its mystique joins hands with technology. But at that time a choice will have to be made. Will it be atheism or the faith?

All roads lead back to this supreme question.

Islam will have to choose between the two poles that are its hallmark. One is Transcendence, by which Islam carries on the tradition of Abraham—the other the flesh and blood that has been its attraction as well as its temptation. Islam has never yet chosen. It has insisted on holding to both contraries without having to choose as the Christians must choose, compelled by the cross which is the symbol of the impossible alliance between Heaven and Earth.

Islam has not wanted to choose between Heaven and Earth. It proposed instead a blending of heaven and earth, sex and mysticism, war and proselytism, conquest and apostolate. In more general terms, Islam proposed a blending of the spiritual and the temporal worlds which neither in Islam nor among the pagans have ever been divided. Islam refused to divide the

Kingdoms and to subordinate the temporal kingdom. Jesus had stated the basic axiom when he had said: 'Give to Cæsar what is Cæsar's, and to God what is God's.' The Cross, which is Separation, and Incarnation, which is Communion, have an essential relation to each other: separation allows true communion. And it is God's absolute transcendence that allowed God's immanence in man by incarnation and by grace.

Can Islam accept this foundation of the Christian mystery, separation between heaven and earth and communion in the Incarnate Word? The specific characteristic of Christ's religion is the synthesis of transcendence and immanence. It asserts the transcendence of the spiritual principle. That principle, on the other hand, is defined as love. History teaches us that it mingled itself in human affairs like a leaven that will now be creative and purifying. There is no doubt that it accepted finitude, took human shape, to a point where it at times became corrupted. And yet it has made the Spirit come down to earth, has built a city and a whole culture of the Incarnation, which differs in principle from the pagan civilizations, and even from that civilization which is Islam's contribution.

Mohammed, we note, radically denies the very essence of Christianity: the love of God, the plurality which is the sign of that love and, consequently, the Incarnation.

Is this denial absolute, or is it merely a difficulty with a small forward step along the road? There are, it seems, men of spiritual power in Islam who today are asking themselves this very question. El Akkad wrote in 1956:

'It is certain that the Christian and the Muslim both follow their deepest religious conviction when they defend, each on his part, their patrimony. Brothers in whom courses the same blood, they have started from common values and taken different paths. The Christian has gone much further. It all comes down to knowing whether one should hold strictly to the fundamental religious values which were those of Abraham and Moses, on pain of falling into blasphemy—as the Muslim believe; or whether God has called men to approach him more closely, revealing to them little by little their fundamental condition as sinful men, and the forgiveness that transforms them and prepares them for the beatific vision—as Christian dogma teaches.'

Catharism

THE MIDDLE AGES WERE NOW AT THEIR HEIGHT. ALL
danger seemed past. Islam lay conquered. Arianism was a thing
of the past. Yet this was the moment when Catholic civilization
was to suffer one of its profoundest crises, from which we have
perhaps not fully emerged to this day.
     What is Catharism? I shall try to define it. I do believe that
the Catharist problem is a supreme problem which every living
conscience and every culture in history must face. It is a problem
which the Church, more surely than any other religious community, was bound to encounter some day. For the Church is
an eternal Idea present in man's time-bound world, it is the
permanent abode of the Word among men, through which the
whole world and all time are drawn toward the eternal kingdom.
     But to understand how intimately opposed the Catharist
spirit is to the Catholic spirit of the Incarnation, we must inquire
more deeply. We must determine what temptation there is
imbedded in the very constitution of the intellect that tends to
dissociate what is indissolubly united in time, and can be separated
only in death.
     There are in reality different planes of existence which,
though distinct *de jure*, are intimately joined *de facto*: body and
mind, flesh and spirit, time and eternity, sex and love, and so on.
Other examples easily come to mind, but these will be enough
to make clear how readily man, feeling that the two values differ
in dignity and function, may be led into the attempt to isolate
and separate the higher part within him, so that he may enjoy it
by itself. Thus he will try to isolate the soul from the body;
to achieve the life of the spirit apart from the body or fragments
of eternity outside of time, to taste and to enjoy them; or again
to isolate certain moments of perfect and so to speak creative
freedom within this life . . . Examples of this dissociation are
readily found. The one closest to us all, and which is least talked
about among men, is that which concerns the ties between flesh
and spirit in sexual life, the dissociation of *eros* and love. It can
be said that human intelligence and industry have at all times

been engaged in dissociating sex from procreation, even from love.

There is concealed beneath all these attempts a metaphysical notion from which they draw their secret energy and sustenance. It is the notion that God the Creator did not stoop to create matter or to involve Himself in it. He was content to cast a few pure sparks into this clay; there has not been a real fusion between the higher element of being and the lower; the foundation of the moral life lies therefore in putting an end to this imprisonment of the pure element within impurity—and to return into the God of utter purity from whom we never have departed in our essential being, despite this earthly adventure of fall and defilement.

Or, to carry the point further, it could be said that these doctrines believe not in a true creation, but rather in an emanation of uncreated light amid a darkness that preceded it; or again, as Simone Weil expressed it at times, that creation is identical with the original sin.

In terms of morality and of freedom, we encounter here once more the Manichaean and gnostic idea that dissociates the inner oneness of the sinner. In this sense *it is impossible for me not to do evil*, since I am matter, the fall, and necessity; but then it is not I who sins but 'I do not know what evil nature', as Augustine said in his Manichaean days. The higher part of ourselves, which remains one with God, cannot commit and does not share in sin.

The study of primitive societies and religions has shown that the separation of the pure from the impure is older than religion, if by religion we mean what the Jews and the Christians meant: a growing communication with God. But even the highest religion preserves similarities with the lowest form of religion because the higher absorbs rather than destroys the lower. We have no right to be surprised if we find the same opposition between the pure and the impure in the Christian religion, its rites and observances, its separation of that which is allowed from that which is forbidden, or of the innocent from the corrupt. One might even say that the image of the Flood and the Ark— the quintessential image of purism which shows an *untouched* element saved from destruction, shipwreck, and defilement—has become indispensable in speaking of election, salvation, or the evangel. The Jewish religion has held on to the image without interruption. It does duty for the mysterious original fault.

Christianity was born in secrecy; it is a victorious conspiracy. The party of Jesus was virtually a conspiracy within Judaism. When this party was immersed within the pagan masses, its methods did not change: the mystic supper, taken in the home for fear of the Jews, had been inaugurated on the first Easter eve.

There have always been in the body of the Church 'parties of the pure' about to rise or to take on new shapes.

The Apostles were the successors of the prophets; they were prophets invested with supreme authority. The moment of Jesus and those He sent was the divine moment of prophetism—the moment when Purity was the power that subdued all. The remarkable thing about the *movement* that started from Jesus is that this moment of purity gave rise to an Institution. The apostolate was succeeded, not by another prophetism but by the Church: the reign of continuity, succession, and the normative institution to which the prophets are subject even more than they were to the Jewish priesthood. Prophets still existed. They came and disappeared without a break. In the time of the Church the 'prophetic office' never ceased. But the prophets rose up and acted within the Church. Their dealings were with the Church. Some were controlled and absorbed by the Church; others were rejected because their purity grew anarchic and threatened the institution.

The Church never was a 'party of the pure'. She sought to achieve not so much perfect purity as purification. Instead, she set up secondary institutions through which a lost purity could be recovered: the offices of forgiveness, penitence, and gradual education.

While the Church extols infinite perfection—*You shall be perfect as your Father in heaven*—she tolerates the existence of a mixed human dough; she knows herself to be a mixed Church, *permixta Ecclesia*. Only God can separate the good from the bad, and as long as time lasts the separation remains uncertain. It can at any time be overturned by the humble conversion of the imperfect, or the fall into pride of the 'perfect' as the example of the good thief or the Apostle turned traitor shows. The separation of the wheat from the chaff will not take place until the last day. Until that day, beneath the appearances which with all their peaks of heroism or of scandal are ambiguous, dim and indifferent, there rule the Divine patience and man's freedom. Absolute purity exists only in the intention. The judgment is not pronounced. Everything is a waiting, a plea, a hope. Such is the time of man with its slow-moving duration and its inextricable mixedness; it is not yet crystalline eternity and its final separation.

We may turn now to certain characteristics of the Albigensian heresy.

It was well-nigh inevitable that the ideal of perfect purity which had given the Church of Christ its start and its drive should appear compromised by reality, and that a counter-Church in the manner of the schools of the Jewish prophets should rise up to reform, to protest, and to save the elect from the corruption which had penetrated into the very sanctuary. All movements of separation, ever since the beginning, have had some such aspect. But it was left to the specific juncture which occurred in the twelfth century in Southern France to carry this ambiguous desire for purity to a point of exaltation and, even more, to the point of inventing an institution which would make that desire a component of Western history, and threaten at once both European civilization and Christianity.

Like all past and future heresies, the Catharist heresy consists not in purism or in laxity, but in a mixture of purism with laxity. Catharism draws the dividing line in the wrong place—between 'spirit' and 'matter', for example, rather than between good will and ill will. It seeks purity in the accidentals rather than in the essence. It tolerates a slackening where it should take a firm stand. In the end, it separates the leaven from the dough. And so the separated leaven loses its power, while the dough must be rejected because it has not been transformed slowly and humbly by the all-embracing effort of the leaven.

Jesus's sermon concerning the Pharisees was meant to show to them that they were seeking an accidental and illusory purity at the expense of essential purity. The Church continues Jesus in the same sense when circumstances call for it.

After repelling the onslaughts of Nordic and Mongol pagans

Catharism

and of Islam, the Church in the eleventh century was gathering strength. But the new doctrine took advantage of this very renewal to establish itself. It started in the East and spread westward. The heretics of this doctrine were known by many names; there were the Paulicians—disciples of Paul of Samosata; the Bogomils and the Buggers (Bulgars); in Italy the heretics were called the Patarenes, after the *Pater* which was their only prayer; in France they took the name of *Cathari*, the Pure.

All these movements drew their strength from the crying abuses of the wealthy and the corruption of some of the clergy—*corruptio optimi pessima*; and from the idea of a return to original simplicity which is always latent in the Church. The twelfth century seems almost to prefigure the sixteenth. There is Peter of Bruys, in Southern France, rejecting infant baptism, the mass, the cult of images, the prayer for the dead, and the celibacy of the priesthood. There is Amaury of Bena, who believed in the eternity of creative matter, and who became the teacher of David of Dinan and William of Paris, the founders of the Brothers and Sisters of the Free Spirit. Even more, there is Peter Waldo, rich burgher of Lyons who sold all his belongings to give to the poor; and who then, poor himself, went out to preach in beard and sandals, and to explicate the gospel in French to all who cared to listen. From him derive the Vaudois or Waldensees who are still called the Poor Men of Lyons, the Humbled, or the *Sabotés* after their footgear. There is, finally, Joachim, the Cistercian abbot of Flora in Calabria, whose disciples proclaimed the coming of a third Time: the first Time was that of the Spouse, the second that of the Priest; the third Time, liberated of the flesh, would be that of the monk, in which the law of the Spirit, the Eternal Gospel, becomes reality.

It is well to recall further that the thirteenth century witnessed those strange phenomena, the 'eschatological returns': thirty thousand poor children on crusade, marching toward God 'through suffering in order to succeed where the great of this world had failed'; those insect plagues which impressed the people of the time as 'a thing unheard-of through all centuries' (1212); and again, around 1251, the uprising of the shepherds, simple young herdsmen who left house and home to attack rich priests, as if to make up for the unworthiness of the élite.

This powerful myth of an uprising of the lowly who will bring about the kingdom of God by their sacrifice is a motif we shall meet again and again. It gave the initial impetus to several crusades. Recast in mundane terms, it reappears in the projects of Saint-Simon and his disciples in the nineteenth century.

All these separate movements, springing up at the same time but independently of each other—they emanated from the collective unconscious, or else were bursts of free invention—had the same end in view concerning the established order and the Church of the Incarnation continued through an institution. They would dissolve the structure in the name of the Spirit who is the author of the structure.

It was not easy to recognize this from the first. But the dissolution of social structures in the twelfth century allowed these movements, essentially anarchic by virtue of their radical purism, to achieve a social status of their own, and thereby to attract the attention of bishops and of popes.

First at Arras in 1025, at Rheims in 1049, Church councils condemned certain doctrinal propositions of a Catharist type.

Little by little the heresy drew together in the South of France. It derived an advantage from the crusades which strengthened the influences from the East, especially in the twelfth century and later. Pope Eugenius III sent a legate to Southern France. St Bernard preached against the heretics. In 1163 a Council held at Tours condemned them under the name of Albigensians. In fact the center of the heresy lay farther to the South, in the plain of the Languedoc. Its capital was Toulouse.

For years the Papacy tried to find a peaceful solution. Its attitude did not change until 1167. The Albigensians, who had by and by organized a counter-Church, held a great council in Toulouse. Most of the lower nobility—that is, the warrior class—were behind them because they saw in the heresy an opportunity to increase their possessions at the expense of Church property. There was, besides, the growing jealousy with which the South of France looked upon the spirit of the North.

In 1194, when Jerusalem had fallen and the Third Crusade collapsed, the Count of Toulouse made common cause with the heretics. The pope, Innocent III, bestirred himself.

To understand the danger that threatened civilization, it will suffice to recall the teachings of the Albigensians.

All sacraments were abolished. In their stead there now was a strange ritual to purify the soul, the 'Consolation'. Marriage was condemned, as was the slaughter of animals, and war. But the supreme, unforgivable fault was to make peace with the Catholic Church. As Hilaire Belloc pointed out, this is one of the principal tenets of every heresy.

It should be noted that the Church was at that time passing through a grave moral crisis. The feudal system was decadent, the towns too rich, the prelates worldly, the clergy debauched; religious indifference was wide-spread, the influence of the East and of Arab philosophy was growing. The Church of the South, sophisticated and frivolous, lacked the faith of the North. Contests in gallant poetry absorbed every mind. 'The priests,' said Peter of Blois, 'had become dogs that could not bark.' The lords were Catharist almost to a man. The convents of the Perfect attracted souls smitten with purity and perfection. 'This is the age of the false friars,' said Hildebert. In short, conditions in the Church foreshadowed those of the sixteenth century at the eve of the Reformation: the scandal aroused the desire for purity, truth, and simplification. They were the best minds who responded to the Catharist call, which was the call for a return to the Church of Jesus, poor, free, not fettered to the state. Catharists and Vaudois opposed the idea of crusade with the 'Thou shalt not kill!' Crusading was to be confined to man's inner struggle. And now, the frightened and sincere souls attracted by the semblance of utter purity were joined by lords in quest of power and envious of the all too visible Church properties. After the nobles came the masses, attracted by the simplicity of the doctrine, with its dualism of good and evil, its rejection of the Incarnation and the principal Christian mysteries, and its local patriotism. The failure of the first several crusades, too, added to general uncertainty.

The crisis was serious; and in this form it had almost no precedent. The other heresies had not threatened the lay civilization, human society, or basic institutions such as marriage, the family, and least of all the instinct to survive. Paganism especially had never known a threat of this nature. Never before had man denied man, except perhaps in certain deviant sects without range, influence, or power. Gnosticism had never in these matters drawn all the conclusions implied in its dualistic principle. Arianism did not attack the foundations of society: on the contrary, it buttressed them with its loyalty to the Emperor. Islam had substituted one dominant race for another, and Africa for Europe; but the human species would have carried on, with Arab blood and the blood of the vassal populations. But the Catharist movement was another matter. Beyond the dogmas and the institution of the Church it was the very roots of the social order, present and future, that were being threatened. The heresy was not just anti-religious but anti-social, anti-laity, a kind of *odium humani generis*. And all this, though it was visible to men of insight, lay concealed under the appearance of its opposite: a reasonable and pure reform; a return to the Church of the Apostles, the practices of the Early Church, and the essence of Christianity.

The spiritual authorities may well have asked themselves whether this new doctrine, with its destructive political and social effects, should not be opposed by force of arms.

Innocent III continued to hesitate until the end of the century. At that time Raymond VI, Count of Toulouse, frightened by dangers threatening from the North, promised to withdraw his support from the heretics and banish their leaders. He was not sincere. St Dominic, who had arrived from Spain, became the moving spirit of the counter-movement. Innocent III used persuasion. He admonished prelates and clergy to do their duty. The Cistercians preached and held public meetings. St Dominic set the example; there were some conversions. But the Albigensian lords organized resistance. In 1208, probably with the connivance of the Count of Toulouse, they arranged the assassination of the Papal legate Peter of Castelnau, Monk of Fontfroide. His dying words were: 'The cause of Christ shall not triumph in this region until one of us sheds his blood for it. Please God that the swords of the persecutor may be the first to stop the killing.'

The assassination prompted Innocent, in keeping with the methods of the time, to organize a 'crusade'. He urged the King of France, suzerain of Toulouse, to resort to force. Soon after, the fighting began.

Leader of the campaign was Simon de Montfort, a lordling from Île-de-France. Philip Augustus had just extended his power by confiscating John Lackland's French dominions. Raymond of Toulouse, fearful that he might be treated the same way, agreed to march with the crusade, but he did so without conviction. He had been excommunicated for the first time in 1207, and had been placed under the feudal ban, later to be reinstated. He was excommunicated once again at Avignon in 1209, first year of real warfare.

The fighting was very bitter. There was mass slaughter and the sacking of towns—Béziers was sacked in 1209. And then came what the pope feared most of all. The Northern lords grew greedy for the riches of the South.

The critical phase of the campaign occurred in 1213. Philip Augustus was for the moment paralyzed by a vast coalition led by John Lackland and supported by the Empire of the Germans. The King of France would be victorious at Bouvines on August 29, 1214. But one year earlier, a great victory of the Northern lords over the Albigensians and their allies prepared Bouvines and made it possible.

Raymond of Toulouse was supported then by an army from Spain, nearly a hundred thousand men led by his brother-in-law, Peter of Aragon, a drunkard and a man of ferocious energy. Peter of Aragon, prompted by the Pope, had proposed to reconcile the opponents. But when negotiations failed, he drew his sword on behalf of his brother-in-law, and Innocent III did not restrain him.

However, the vast army from Aragon combined with the Albigensian forces formed a disorganized mass, and its mounted men were in the minority. Simon de Montfort, after hearing mass sung by St Dominic, routed the whole Aragonese army near Muret by a sudden charge in the early hours of September 13, 1213. A thousand men fought against forty thousand, and slew twenty thousand.

The battle of Muret is one of those decisive encounters when the fate of the world hangs in the balance. Most historians, strange to say, ignore this fact. Without this most improbable victory of Muret, Bouvines would not have been possible. The French monarchy was all but ruined, the triumph of the new doctrine nearly certain. In fact, the Albigensians dominated the richest and best organized lands in all the West. They had the highest culture, and their great port of Narbonne controlled the commerce of the Mediterranean Sea. Whatever example they set would have been followed.

The people of the North had won. Half of the South lay in ruins. The battle of Muret laid the foundation of the French monarchy, prevented the destruction of the medieval civilization of the thirteenth century, and so allowed it to go on, into the civilization of the West.

The Albigensian heresy was attacked not just by force of arms —civil and ecclesiastical institutions also fought against it. The Inquisition was born of the need to extirpate the remnants of the heresy. As we sit in judgment over this tribunal with its frightful excesses, we must take account not only of the mentality of the Middle Ages; we must also measure the horror of the remedy by the horror of the disease.

The Albigensian peril was repelled at the price of savage measures and terrible destruction. At that price humanity, even more than Christianity, was no doubt saved from sacred suicide.

The philosophical arsenal of Catharism consisted of this dualism of good and evil, eternal and temporal, mind and matter, whose absurdity makes us realize the importance of not separating the two by force in this preparatory, enigmatic, and probationary phase that we call history. The *Cathari* once again took up the Gnostic and Manichaean theme. God has created the universe of perfect men, free men, 'good men'; the evil god has created matter, and many spirits have been caught in this muck. Jesus is an angel come to save them, but has a body only in appearance, a body that was not born, and that died only in appearance. He passed through this fading semblance only to teach us that one must renounce the earth, the flesh, and life itself.

In his image, now, the Pure will detach themselves radically from all things: they will not know the use of property or of marriage, for use and abuse are the same. As soon as one makes use of anything one is lost, and may as well go to the limit of excess. The Pure will be saved at death. This death, however, to which one must look forward so much, they may anticipate by mystic suicide, either by poisoning or starving themselves to death.

The Perfect Ones are initiated by a sacrament called *Consolamentum*, a kind of confirmation. They alone are true Christians.

However, the Catharists realized that perfection could be only for a very few. Accordingly their doctrine was full of indulgence for the human condition. Every faithful was potentially perfect, perfect in expectancy and in desire. They were all like Emperor Constantine, who because of his crimes could not assume the moral obligations of baptism until the hour of his death; or like certain orthodox Russians who enter into their religion on their dying day, and have themselves buried in a monk's habit. So the Catharists ingeniously solved the problem of perfection by delaying it to that moment when the soul has no more time. They let themselves be initiated, 'consoled', at the last moment. But after that, one had to die. If he did not, he had to stop being a *believer* and become a Perfect One. Those who returned from the brink of death sometimes took poison to avoid a relapse, or were hurried along to their salvation by zealous relatives who starved them to death.

Meantime the rank and file of the faithful, perfect only in hope, were content to live on the level of 'believers'. Believers could permit themselves the use of things, even human abuse. They married. E   since the works of the flesh were evil in a marriage that brought children, it was better for them to use the flesh outside of marriage. So long as they were not perfect they could go to the limit of imperfection. The believers placed themselves outside the bounds of society. They had to refuse the oath because it would have bound them to society, that work of Satan. On the same grounds they had to avoid military service.

There is no liturgy to parallel the Catholic cult, no images, no cross. Instead there is a weekly rite in which the Paternoster only is recited, an *agape* where everyone present receives the sacred bread to take home; and a confession of a kind called *appareillamentum*.

The seductive power of such a doctrine, such a morality, and such an institution can well be understood. In its way it solved the problem of the obligation to be perfect which troubles every Christian conscience. It came to terms with weakness.

The Catholic Church had followed a vastly different path: she had called all the faithful to the perfection of charity and love. She had permitted and encouraged schools of perfection, where those who felt the call to leave all things might train themselves in this free and absolute sacrifice for the good of all. Even as she urged everyone *to rise higher*, the Catholic Church came to the aid of every sinner to offer him the means of reconciliation, of re-education, and of mercy with ever open arms. Hence, there was no caste of perfection in society, and no moments of absolute perfection in the individual's life, nor moments of despair. Everything remained in a state of impulsion, regret, and love. No one could tell which man had the greatest love. The perfect might be rotten with a subtle pride, the imperfect redeemed and saved by generous humility. A difficult path, which reconciled contraries by maintaining each respectful of the other, in loving peace, in unquiet hope. Thus was realized even in this world the *communio sanctorum*, the communion of saints, and yet no one was ever proclaimed a saint, no sinner ever condemned.

The Catharist solution was less difficult. It made the problem disappear without in fact solving it. Under the appearance of fervor, rigor, and asceticism—and also of humaneness, compassion, and kindness—it followed down the evil inclines of human nature. At bottom it was wonderfully easy. The existence of the Perfect Ones was reassuring. The idea that on the last day one could finally be one of the Perfect Ones sanctioned constant failures and even frenzied evil. For it assured the 'believer' that his condition inevitably implied such failures; besides, the sacrifice of the Perfect Ones made up for them; and finally, even the impure were pure by virtue of that sincere desire which they would show on drawing their last breath. Thus one could have the advantages which evil offers on earth, and the eternal advantage of salvation after death.

A moralist will say that we are all Catharists even though we do not know it; for all of us aspire toward a morality so permissive and so promising that it could make us citizens both of the world and of heaven, both slaves of evil and servants of God. Catharism skilfully sanctified this shamefaced and pure desire of our incompetent consciences. A study of the thoughts and practices of the Catharists is today like a metaphysical and moral experiment that shows up the ambiguities in any search for purity without sacrifice.

This dissociation of the pure part of ourselves from the impure appears nowhere so clearly as in the Catharist solution of the problem of sex, the greatest unnamed heresy of the West.

It was an old dream of gnosticism to justify at one stroke both asceticism and the orgy.

A fragment of the *Gospel According to the Egyptians*, a gnostic writing of the second century preserved by Clement of Alexandria, supplies the following dialogue:

To Salome who asked how much time the time of death would last, the Lord said: As long as you women will give birth to children. And Salome said to him: I have done well, then, not to have children. The Lord answered her: Eat of all the fruits, but of that which is bitter thou shalt not eat. Salome having asked him how this should be understood, the Lord answered: When you cast off the vestment of shame, the body, and when the two shall be one—the male and the female—there will no longer be man nor woman.

If matter is essentially evil we must renounce its deeds, its works, we must abstain, must die to return to life outside of matter. Marriage of the flesh then is a mortal sin, and there is no real difference between marriage, adultery, and incest. *Matrimonium est lupanar.*

But matters can be arranged. Suppose a man were sufficiently in control of his senses to be his own master in the lap of pleasure, free not to yield to the desire to beget man which is the urge of the flesh; suppose he had sufficiently disciplined his senses or his technique not to give in to procreation, that work of Satan— then what is to prevent him from enjoying the flesh which is now dispossessed and rendered harmless? The act and its enjoyment take place below the realm of conscience, which remains pure, rapt in contemplation, disengaged. All the more so because, if there remains some element of sin in this surrender to the flesh, it is a small sin compared with the sin of the creator who gave way to the point of making the flesh proliferate, and so condemned us to the generations.

All this helps us to understand how such a morality could justify excesses of contraception and unnatural vices. It both made use of, and hastened, the movement of despair which rushes on to the extremes of evil when it feels incapable of the extremes of good. He who does not feel capable of the highest is automatically empowered to surrender to the lowest. If he cannot live continently, then let him enjoy himself as he may, provided he does not beget children. Catharist morality knows only the two extremes, the absolutely Pure and the absolutely Impure. It aims at the one and forgives the other, condemning only the middling, bourgeois way of life, which is the way of human life and of the multitudes.

Thus logic leads us straight into the supreme absurdity: the negation of all moral responsibility and every stable society. Dualism here holds out its bitter fruit. If the Good remains the Good even in the midst of evil, if there is no possibility of failure because the pure cannot to any degree become involved in the impure, then man is dissociated forever: he is no longer a moral conscience, but a team: he is angel and beast, each sovereign on its level.

Thus, as the *Gospel of Salome* has it—and its echo can be heard in the *Gospel of Thomas* recently found in the sands of Egypt—the union of man and woman in barren orgasm becomes the supreme act, the first androgynous being, the divine form.

Courtly love drew on this metaphysical morality, translating it into acceptable terms.

According to the most recent interpreters, Lavaud and Nelli, only the lady who had already known carnal love could, if she so desired, enter the realm of pure love. This explains the indifference of medieval literature to the position of the young maid. Her virtue and her courtesy became of interest only when she was capable of being unfaithful. Marrou says with good reason that courtly love was by definition adulterous.

Denis de Rougemont, author of many searching studies on the subject, sees in this courtly phenomenon the *psychic revolution of the twelfth century*, a wide-spread feature of the history of civilization. He finds analogies in sixth century India with its

Tantra Buddhism, and in the Mathayoga of Hinduism. We know that *Tantra* chastity consists in seeking the ecstasy of the mind and the senses through a chosen woman whom one does service in a position of subjection, without ever begetting offspring. It is the same idea as that love in languor, servitude and intellectual fire sung by the Arab poets and the troubadours, from which the West derives a certain notion of Woman adored in adultery. It is a doctrine unknown to Antiquity which thought little of woman, and is altogether contrary to the Jewish idea and Christian doctrine of married union.

In opposition to these errors, the cult of the Virgin greatly grew in strength. Confronting the danger of degenerate courtly love, the Virgin is the symbol of true purity raised to the level of the sublime. Her cult offered an antidote to the false cult of woman by giving it an object of adoration that is worthy of it. As Auguste Comte said, it was a civilizing and ordering dogma.

I have said that there is a kind of Eternal Catharism whose traces may be found wherever mysticism turns into a human technique, as it did in India, in Greece, and among the gnostics. Let me be precise: this Catharism is ever ready to arise at the point where heart and body are joined. In principle, Catharism is an escape from evil, not by repentance and purification but by dividing the self in two. Who would not want to be Catharist in order to *deliver himself from evil* without penance and without having to face the Judge? And who does not turn Catharist at certain moments of failure, protesting all that is noble and pure in him against that which he is but does not want to be?

After the end of the Albigensians, the civilization of the West, proceeding along the course of time, has shown unpredictable forms of Catharism.

Puritanism is one of these—more respectable, more institutional, and somehow grown in wisdom. The Puritan is a double being, not a man who sacrifices himself. I mean to say that he achieves the unity of his being not by that act of mortification which makes the impure in us subservient to the pure. He achieves a seeming unity and peace by leaving his inferior part to its own laws of the flesh and self-interest, pleasure or profit, but compensating for that concession by a mask of austerity, false modesty, and rigor. The Puritan is more severe on his neighbor and purer of face and speech in proportion as his true morals are more secret. This, at any rate, would be prototype of that 'puritan' conduct which carries to an extreme the temptation felt by every devoted 'honest man', every firm Christian.

With the Puritan, and his European counterpart, the 'bourgeois', being and appearance are dissociated: he is the very definition of hypocrisy. But as happens with so many revolts, Catharist hypocrisy brings forth Catharist laxity; we in Europe have often seen how the hatred of the false face can reach a pitch where the mask is flung off and with it every notion of restraint, where cynicism seems preferable to hypocrisy. Remember André Gide. But puritanism and amoralism belong to the same species: both are extremes. One and the other presupposes a certain dualism of Good and Evil, Being and Appearance. One and the other adopts the moral rule of division in two: the beast is on the ground floor, the angel one flight up. A man who has not sacrificed himself is dissociated without being united—like the Docetist Christ who, while God on his own level, is born, lives, suffers and dies in appearance only.

A form of Catharism might have arisen in the eighteenth century and even in our own. But before a heresy turns from a possibility into a fact, a combination of circumstances is needed, among which the most important is political appeal. However, in Europe there could not exist any political force that would be interested in promoting a new radical Catharism such as that of the 'Bonshommes'. Besides, the civil laws would not have permitted it, and the Perfect Ones would quickly have found themselves in jail. We need to recall only how we Europeans deal with those who refuse to bear arms. The Catharist crisis will certainly never return in that form. Seen in this light it is a sort of *hapax*, a most improbable one-time event made to lead historian-philosophers astray.

After a heresy is crushed, especially if it is crushed by terror, these things remain behind: the precautions that were taken to keep it from returning; the institutions in which survives what remained valid; and finally, the secret movements in which the heresy lives on toward the day when it will re-emerge—often more effective than before.

Catharism

The Catharist experience confirmed the Church in her chosen path. It did not prompt the Church to grow suspicious of virginity, asceticism, detachment from worldly goods, or true purity. It could be said that the Church on the contrary desired more than ever to show that she was the true virginal bride: in the thirteenth century the cult of purity blossomed in the West. I have mentioned how it pervades that devotion to Mary which is so characteristic of Catholic piety. This is not the first time that we witness the operation of that mysterious and subtle law by which a vanquished heresy helps to develop the devotion to Mary. It almost seemed as though there were a secret link between the Idea of the Virgin-Mother and Catholic orthodoxy; Karl Barth might agree with me here. We should understand the matter better if every heresy had (as I believe it has) a direct or indirect bearing upon the Incarnation to which the Mother of the Christ-God is so closely linked.

The Albigensian crisis may be said to have enabled the papacy to approve the works of Francis and Dominic, those two new prophets for the new times. Seen from outside, there is no great difference between a Friar Minor and a Perfect One: they exhibit the same absolute detachment from everything including marriage, the same 'perfect' joy, and similar peculiarities of dress. But Francis does not reproach those whose vices he deplores. He does not boast of his purity. He looks toward his bishop and toward Rome. He asks for papal approbation. He tries to incarnate the aspiration toward total poverty during man's imperfect existence within this poverty-stricken world. After founding the two orders of the Friars Minor and the Sisters, he established the Third Order of the Brothers and Sisters of Penitence for this very purpose. Comparing the performance of Francis with that of one of the Perfect Ones, the little difference reveals a vast chasm between one and the other.

Dominic, although he lived in Catharist country, and also, no doubt, for that very reason, did not strive to resemble the Catharists so as to beat them on their own ground, as Francis did. His activity was less spectacular and less popular. He attacked the head, the Catharist teaching. He brought no innovations but adopted the rule of St Augustine. But in the end, following the example of the Franciscans, he desired no other riches than the virtue of his brothers; and so the possessions of his order were distributed among the poor. Such were the first two begging orders, the mendicants; not separated from the world but living among people, a kind of regenerated knighthood which under the impulsion of the popes restored Jesus's spirit within the Church. Now an amazing thing happened. Although (and many an 'although' is a 'because') the sons of Francis and the sons of Dominic had renounced all things, there awakened in their midst the love of learning and of study, even of books—which makes ownership necessary.

The strength of a king, especially a French king, lies in attaching to himself the fiefholders who revolted, and to create a nobility; a nobleman, after all, is a critic won over. In the same way, it was the strength of the Church, after the scandals of her impurity and the repression of the false Pure Ones, that she brought forth these beggar-monks, the Orders of the dispossessed. The disciples of St Francis and St Dominic are, so to speak, Catharists purified and in submission—they are the Catharists of the Church. Excess of evil does at times bring about the renewal of the Good; and the Church recovers and adds to her own stature what was just and pure and true among those who opposed her. Newman remarked of St Thomas that he had restored the truth implied in Aristotle, the same Aristotle whom the early Fathers had denounced as the sum of all unbelief and especially of the Arian and monophysite heresies.

Though Catharism has been crushed by the secular power; though it has been sublimated in the mendicant orders; though in the thirteenth and fourteenth centuries a purified Catharism has inspired medieval civilization at its height—yet it lives on in the bloodstream of the great body of Christianity, all the more present and active because now, left without means of expression, it is to some degree forced underground.

It is obvious that we shall meet Catharism again at the source of the Reformation. It may even be that the surge of indignation and the drive for purity which set off the Reformation arose from those very failures of the Church to the South which had been contained by the partial reform of Innocent III and the saintly founders of the new Orders; and which had risen up again in the days of the Reformation in a form that was less radical and more theological, more human, and more political.

The great difficulty in every movement of purification is not to make a break. He who breaks, destroys—he does not purify. That is the difference between the reformer and the saint, between the Catharist and the truly pure.

There have at all times been men of high courage who have stood up in the face of abuse and denounced it. In Israel, the agitation of the prophets to restore the Purity of Tradition had become almost a permanent feature of public life. When the prophetic voice fell silent, it seemed as though God had withdrawn. The prophetic function was continued within the Church; the founders of religious orders, united to the Holy See, symbol and guarantor of unity, handed on the prophetic influence and the presence of a magistracy of purification.

It would seem that the 'prophetic office' has in modern times passed more and more out of the hands of the clergy into those of the laity. This function of the prophetic clarion call is at times even assumed by the unbeliever denouncing institutional vices with all the ancient vigor of the prophets. In their full independence of the religious powers, at times even in revolt against them, these modern prophets do not constitute a solid body as the ancients did; there are gaps in the sequence. The only demand they make on the temporal or spiritual, political or sacerdotal powers is the very opposite of a demand for support: they call for condemnation. They need this paradoxical investiture. But the pure of our age, Catharist in more than one respect, blend with the partisans, and the partisans with the negators. It is not easy to determine whether this desire to be pure does not spring from a revulsion, a secret desire to reduce to nothingness the very thing whose impurity shocks you. If so, the negative partisan spirit is something altogether different from the search for purity. Purity implies the very opposite of the wish to destroy: the desire to see the thing one wants to purify have a fuller existence, to lead it back to its essence by a discreet, patient, and continuous effort that condemns no one, since no one knows before the end of time where eternal purity resides. True, if one has grown up within a minority that is dispossessed, or thinks it is; if one has suffered to the point of death from the scandal of the élite; then it is difficult not to reach out for purity even by way of negation. The obstacle is such a torment, it does not leave us truly free with regard to it. We see it before our eyes and are deluded by it. Looking about us with the eyes of resentment and of passion, we come to take for bad faith whatever is not a faith calling for perfect purity, to take for alienation whatever is not absolute freedom, and for nothingness whatever is not self-created conscience. At that stage, Catharism is the supreme temptation.

The same problem arises in the modern conflict between the flesh and the mind. Modern man tries to dissociate the flesh from the mind; and next, to put an end to the division, he tries now to smother the flesh, now again to join it to the mind. It is true, of course, that the battle between the flesh and the mind has always been the hardest of human experiences. But paganism, amorism, Romanticism were content to deify the *Eros*, by turning passion into something like a baptism that renders all things holy —much as does pain, pain of which *Eros* seems to be the burning counterpart. In our age we feel it more than ever—for we are more mind than flesh—that the unity of the flesh with the mind is man's fundamental problem. But how difficult a problem it is for the intellect! The Romantic solution makes us smile. The point at issue is not to surrender to instinct, even deified instinct. The point is to taste pleasure to the full, either by despising or by sublimating it, while one's inner purity is never lost, in fact, grows . . . This is the Catharist theme appearing once again, but this time in a context of extreme sophistication. The idea is still that the higher part of ourselves is not involved in the adventure of sex, not even in sexual perversions; and that purification is gained not by struggling but by living apart, on a higher plane. Homosexuality, which existed among the Arabs in Catharist times and which has reappeared more cynically in modern times, has always carried the dissociation of pleasure and function to the extreme. It surely was familiar to those falsehoods of Catharist purity which, in the days of the troubadours as in the days of Narcissus and Swann, gave rise to works of beauty by a kind of diabolical accident.

The Churches that have risen against the Roman Catholic Church in the course of history have seen their justification in the idea that they were 'purer than' or 'the only pure'. Anglicanism and Donatism show profound similarities in this regard; a realization of these analogies was the first cause of Newman's conversion. The modern revolutions which introduced religious concepts into the political order (from where they had been carefully banished by the Christian kings) have celebrated the idea of the Pure Ones in the Party Member. That idea of false purity has invaded the collective consciousness. The 'Occupying Power' of the most recent wars has been understood not just in the categories of master and servant, but in the more ancient, more religious, and more sexual category of the defiler. A Frenchman who has lived through the two wars needs only to compare the levels of aversion against the enemy to realize how vast the difference has grown. The Catharist idea has remained alive in the relations between empires; Russia and America alike think of themselves in these terms today. One might say that in the ways in which men judge each other and themselves, the concepts of the Pure and the Impure carry more weight in our times than those of Good and Evil—and our consciences generally translate Good and Evil into Pure and Impure. Every man looks on his neighbor in terms of these two concepts that are always at hand, and one feels that no-one's position in the estimation of his neighbours is so secure that he might not be shifted from Pure to Impure.

Our reflection on the terrible Albigensian episode might lead us to understand the full ambiguity of this short word Pure, so attractive in its soft, quick sound. In one way it recalls what to each one of us is his most secret and most sublime desire: to be Pure, unclouded, detached, strong enough even to contemplate defilement, and also to be capable of that movement which both annihilates and sublimates, the movement in which Hegel saw the driving power of history. But true purity is a difficult thing, for it is often destroyed at the root the very instant it is proclaimed, the instant one believes to possess it unalloyed. True purity can never be separated from the humble and persistent striving for a self-purification that is never attained; it can never be separated from a universal love for all men, high or low, involved in matter and in failure, who grieve that they are not pure. We cannot stop time, put an end to mixture, deny the Incarnation, secure admission to eternity. We must wait for death. The Catharist wants to run ahead of death.

The Protestant Reformation

WE NOW TURN TO THAT PERIOD OF TIME WHICH EXTENDS from the end of the Middle Ages to our own day. It is a difficult period to define and describe because we are ourselves a living part of it.

One could project upon that time span the image of the present, of the era in which we have been living for the last ten years. For in both instances we are witnessing the birth of a new age. Every birth is ambivalent. One never knows whether he is stepping on a seed that holds the future, or on a piece of wreckage from the past—whether the vision is a monstrous dream or the shape of things to come. I well remember those 'airplanes' of my childhood, puffing and shaky kites too heavy to stay aloft. Men are blind to the new beginnings of their own day. The new birth slips in quietly and surely, and takes hold in the substance of things. When its opponents want to stop it, it is too late. The pagan emperors persecuted too late, and so the nascent Church took root.

And there is something else even stranger. Inventors—such as Gutenberg, Papin, or Edison—hardly foresaw the extent of the transformation they had started. They were outdistanced by their own world-wide success. Besides, the invention of printing, of the steam engine, electricity, or the rocket is in itself not enough to work those sudden changes: the Chinese had invented gun-powder and the compass, but did not benefit from their inventions. Invention had to coincide with a certain state of men's minds, a virtual hunger that demanded to be stilled. Only such an underlying condition explains how a spark that falls on ready ground can almost instantaneously set off an explosion.

Neither St Paul nor Arius nor Mohammed nor Lenin had expected the conflagration. In each case it was due most of all to the specific combination of conditions, to the meeting of a material cause—the unrest and needs and resentments of a multitude of men—with a spiritual and mystic cause which is at bottom always a new form of hope.

But to return to the crisis of the Protestant Reformation with which I am here dealing: we must grant that neither Erasmus nor Luther nor Calvin had any notion of the transformation they would bring about. They said repeatedly that they had no intention to dissociate the Church from Christ—only to reform her, to guide her back to her sources, so to speak, and make her young again.

The case is altogether different with Communism, which had been foreseen by Karl Marx, lone strategist, long before it surged up. The case is altogether different also for the revolution which St Paul brought about in such full and triumphant awareness.

A great age could have been born at that time. The world stopped closing itself in upon the little space of the inland sea, and the time of the Jews and Christians. The twofold discovery of antiquity and of a 'New World' threw open new dimensions in space and in time. In our day, too, perspectives are immeasurably and doubly enlarged: by telescope, spectral analysis, the imminence of interplanetary missiles, and the simultaneous discoveries of Peking Man and the 'pre-hominids'. But these things have in a sense been foreseen, or at least were foreseeable to the trained eye. The only real innovation would be the discovery of another thinking species on another planet. What an upheaval in all our ways of thought and feeling that would mean! The sixteenth century, now, witnessed a vaguely analogous phenomenon.

By one of those paradoxes to which we are inured by history— what happens is so often the reverse of what we did expect—the Church did not extend herself into these two dimensions of space and time. Instead she contracted at first, in self-defence. One has the impression of a great missed opportunity. But time is the arena of failure, and of those things we call *defeat* which herald sublime compensations of another order.

In those days of explosive expansion the Latin, virtually Catholic, religion had a chance to show itself capable of extending to the All. Only a regrouping was necessary, then an expansion; the one would follow from the other. It did not happen. The humanists offered a most reasonable solution. Several eminent minds Catholic both in origin and in desire—such as Montaigne, Rabelais, Descartes and, more generally, the great Jesuit teachers

—proposed to continue the direction of the Middle Ages, with more stress on ancient languages and the classical spirit that was having its renaissance in the print shops. Among minds that would henceforth be divided in faith and tempted to indifference, the humanist solution would have tended to create a common ground of language, tone, and culture and if need be of human heroism, where Catholicism could take root. The European ideal, ambiguous ideal, would be of this kind—from Corneille to Voltaire and to Chateaubriand, and even to Barrès. But once a conscience or a culture has been infused with Christianity, it cannot ever again return to an earlier age that seems more spacious, more indifferent, *without denying Christianity* at first in fact, later in principle; it cannot return to a state of 'nature' or of 'reason' like that of the Greeks or even of the Jews before Christ. A full-grown man cannot return to inarticulate and fresh childhood without risking infantilism. The flow of time cannot be reversed. Our ship is headed toward the high sea. Deism or humanism in the post-Christian era will not be like the deism or humanism of antiquity. Modern deism and humanism must inevitably follow the fateful decline that ends up in an anthropocentric religion opposed to traditional Christianity.

At the end of the Middle Ages, thoughtful people felt that a reform of the wide-spread abuses was a necessity. The sudden contact with classical culture helped to discern what was worth preserving in the medieval complex.

We know what happened. The Church could not reform itself in time, or did not know how to do it. The Reformation movement rose up in opposition to the Church, and led to the secession of large numbers of believers—first parties, then whole nations. It can be said that Catholicism retained no more than a semblance of Romanism. South Germany, Austria, and Poland remained Catholic, or else returned to Catholicism. So did the Empire itself. But the Anglo-Saxon and Germanic countries cut themselves off from the Roman center, just as the vast Slavic expanses had done in the ninth century. The secession was not just a separation, a simple rending of the cloth, like that of the Christian East in the days of Photius, which had produced a Catholic Church separate from Rome that was called *orthodox*. This time,

the new Christians looked upon the very structure of the Church
—her dogma, hierarchy, and priesthood, her idea of salvation,
her liturgy, in short the whole Catholic Church—as the Church
of the Anti-Christ, not that of Christ.

It was as though the time of the Apocalypse had returned.
The Rome of the popes stood in the place of the Beast of Babylon.
Reformed Christianity spread rapidly throughout Europe; its
colonization peopled North America; the great intellectual
centers of the world, other than Rome, Madrid, and Paris, were
in the camp of the Reformers, not of Rome. Leaving theology
and science to one side, several great cultural movements—
Hobbes, Locke, Hume, Rousseau, Hegel, the masters of systematic
organizing thought—applied the ideas of Luther and Calvin to
the political order, bringing about absolutism in one place,
democracy in another. Kant, in his defiance of reason like a
secular Luther, advanced a new way of philosophizing which
would make of man first the center of being, next the center
of becoming. One might say also that the criticism of the Christian
origins, and the historical criticism of dogma, were born in
Germany's Protestant theological faculties. The great wars of
the nineteenth and twentieth centuries were religious wars, either
among the nations emancipated and the old Catholic nations,
or among the enemy brothers, the Germans and the English.

France, whose dynasty, people, and thinkers remained faithful
to Rome, was not transformed from top to bottom by the Reformation. Like Clovis this powerful and improbable event shaped
the course of history. If we imagine Louis XVI a Protestant, or
Gallican in the sense in which Henry VIII was Anglican, the
Revolution of 1789, if it had taken place at all, would not have
been so anti-religious. The head of the last Capetian would surely
not have rolled. Could there have been a Napoleon? How
different France and all of Europe would be today!

How are we to understand that effects so universal, so general,
and apparently so durable, should come from the experiences
and the impetuosity of one pious monk—even granting that he
possessed that rare combination of a mystical with a practical
genius, and that he enjoyed the connivance of various circumstances?

To my mind this is one of the enigmas of Western history.

The Protestant Reformation

The difficulty is more or less neglected by both sides, because it troubles both sides. Any disproportion between cause and effect is troublesome to the mind—it constitutes a failure of the mind's supreme principle of explanation. Catholics cannot explain to themselves this unimaginable disaffection with which so many Catholics, sixteen hundred years after the birth of Jesus, seemed to reject, even deny the immense accumulated labors of those who had preceded them in the faith. The Protestants themselves, with all their exaltation over so vast a success in the world, feel somewhat embarrassed, because they cannot hide from themselves the fact that their revolution in the name of purity has been supported by some very impure forces.

We are here faced again with that theologico-political phenomenon of which I spoke on several occasions. But this time it assumed unparalleled proportions—proportions co-extensive with all culture and civilization. This collusion of the two causes has lent a certain ambiguity to the rise and expansion of the world of the Reformation. For it makes the Reformation seem similar to the other heresies known to history—at least on first sight.

In fact, we here encounter once again the hidden rhythm, the living dialectic of the great revolutions of consciences in revolt. We see their scandal at abuse, their intransigence, their purity, their inflexibility, their willingness to accept the worse in order to save the true, their hope of a new start in Christianity. We also see their anguish, their inner fragmentation, their fatal alliance with others who are less pure, and finally the impossibility of their return to that first stage when their innovation was still a development and a reform which were acceptable and desirable within the Church.

The Reformation stemmed from a premature despair with the all too visible failures of the Church, and from the growth of an extreme sensitivity to the decadence of power, theology, and the cult. Men would have needed an excess of faith and hope, not to be crushed by the certain prospect that in time corruption would destroy what was most sublime. In the sixteenth century, corruption, ironically and scandalously, appeared precisely in those high places where an example should have been set: the Roman Curia and the monasteries; it appeared in those acts that should have been sacred: penitence, indulgence, the inter-

149

cession of the Virgin and the Saints, the application of Christ's Passion in the reiteration of the mass. But the surprise, the sacred horror bordering on dread at the abuses that had entered the very sanctuary—always one of the great stimulants of prophetic protest—does not lead with necessity to schism and condemnation. It may on the contrary inspire penitence, 'reform', a recourse to suffering so as to bear witness and to redeem. The saints, who suffer from such miseries more deeply than do others, ask God at times to visit the punishment for such defilement upon their own purity. One may well say that the problem of abuse, reform, and reparation has been a constant element in the Church, and has called forth unceasing reforms, and a return to the evangel that was the burning desire of the great founders of the religious order.

But guided by the mind of Luther, the Reformation turned into something quite other than a return to the right road. Luther cast doubt upon the traditional faith; he did not lower its level, as Marcion, Montanus, Arius, or Pelagius had found it possible to do. On the contrary, Luther raised the general level by exalting the All-Power, the All-Freedom, the All-Essence, the All-Sovereignty of God and of His gifts, and granting *nothing* to man's freedom. *Sola fide!* If Protestantism is a heresy it is, in terms of dogma, a heresy of maximism.

On the other hand, the Reformation released the Catholic in practice from his Church obligations, and therewith from the system of the sacraments which the Church had established on the authority of Jesus Christ. In particular, it released the faithful from auricular confession and from all ecclesiastical penitence; it reduced the part played by what Renan called the 'daily supernatural'. It gave to the believer all freedom in the interpretation of Scripture. Simple believers who were not theologians gained the impression that their practical life had undergone a liberation. The lowly could read and pray as they pleased. Princes could free themselves of the Pope, and could divorce. And the property of the Church was free for the taking.

There was a counter-balancing, an oscillation, a compensating action between the two levels. The rigor and exclusiveness that had been added on the side of dogma by the idea of the all-sufficiency and all-might of faith alone, of grace alone, of God

Alone and His free and terrible judgments—all this was counter-balanced by what was taken away from the common duties in matters of obedience, ritual, and various injunctions. Set free from a Catholicism that had been judged too narrow, the Christian soul could by a rapid back-and-forth find reassurance in these new liberties, which it desired for the sake of independence, even while it dreaded them in a vague remorse. If the Christian made free with the rules of sex, the subordination of pastor to bishop or of council to pope, and with the freedom to believe, he could in return tell himself that he was free of self-interest and superstition in his adoration of the Savior God Who does not look to merit, Who is the sole cause of sanctity or damnation, Who 'guides our will and deed within us according to his will', as the Apostle Paul had said.

I would say further that the belief in radical predestination, which might have been expected to paralyze all effort and make men despair of salvation, did on the contrary lend wings to the joy of action and daring enterprise. We have seen before in history how doctrines at whose center stands necessity do in effect liberate: among Stoics, and again only yesterday among the Scientists of whom Taine made himself the spokesman. The reason is that the belief in necessity is never quite as intimate or all-embracing as one might think. At the decisive moment we always make an exception for ourselves, just as we never think of ourselves as mortal. The belief in fatality frees us of remorse, regret, and fear; it also frees us of that awful obligation which is ours, to judge our fellow-man before the inner judge; and even more it frees us of the anguished uncertainty that wells up in us out of the thought that events, and people, and finally our own selves might in truth be other than they are. A good Jansenist will admit that someone else is predestined for hell, but not he; he never thinks sincerely that he might himself go to hell. In short, even within the hardest and most hopeless doctrines we think of ourselves as saved, in spite of all and everything; which gives us the delightful feeling of almost boundless freedom. What is hardest is at times what is most reassuring, just as the excellent takes less trouble than the mediocre. The reason is that we do not push hardness to its final logical conclusions. There are compensations.

The counter-balancing oscillation showed itself in another area as well. The fathers of the Reformation would have been horrified if they could have foreseen the prodigious extensions of Protestantism. The first reformers were hostile to the culture of the humanistic, rational and classical kind that was taking root in Europe. They wanted to preserve the Christians from the world's corruption, from the contagion of profane knowledge, from that medieval philosophy which was so reasonable and so fond of reasoning, from every trace of that bastard mixture of the pagan with the evangelical spirit of which the Rome of the Popes was for them the symbol.

The intention of the fathers of the Reformation, as that of every reformer, was to save an island of purity, a rock of the elect, a holy ark, a walled-in city of uncontaminated faith, and to set up and maintain limited models here and there to serve as signs and guideposts, as the Puritans of the *Mayflower* would do later, or those little 'congregations' of the Quakers which Voltaire mentions with such admiration in his *Letters on the English Nation*. These preserves of the Spirit would fill the rôle of the medieval monasteries, but without their disadvantages. The first Protestants did not favor the idea of missions, either because the apostolate had been completed by the Apostles, or else because all missionary zeal was indiscreet, since God had fixed the number of his elect. What mattered was to preserve the universe of the Word, the enclave of the Spirit.

But the new world was being born outside of medieval Christianity—a world of exploration and discoveries, daring and enterprise, a world of finance and investment, Atlantic fleets, new and self-governing nations, of commerce, of money with its exchange and its risks; a world of nascent liberties in which serfs wanted to be free, princes to be kings, kings to be independent of Empire and Holy See. It was like a new mutation of the species. Our own age with its colonial emancipation around the world may serve as an analogy.

Would the young Protestantism lock itself up in its Ark, its Patmos, its catacombs? Or would it offer itself to that world in ferment? If it did offer itself, would it be to call the world back to the ancient order and to discipline—or, on the contrary, to urge it on in its new ways? What, for example, would Calvinist casuistry have to say on the uses of money, the 'lending at interest' which had been generally condemned by medieval theologians; or on the heretofore imprescriptible law concerning the indissolubility of marriage?

The Catholic Church, too, would be faced with this problem of how to adapt herself to unforeseeable conditions in the world. She solved it, it seems, in keeping with the ancient prudence which detests extremes, maintaining the difference between *counsel* and *precept*, at times by means of subtle casuistry. But Protestantism, we note, joined vigorously in the game of that same world which it condemned as the abode of the Evil One, either because it had accepted the world from the outset, or else because it was drawn into it against its will.

Again we witness the secret power of compensation. The purer the Protestant doctrine was in its essence, its reform, its hopes, and in certain of its expressions such as the city-Church Geneva under Calvin—the more this ardent, living, liberated faith, simplified and stripped of all ballast, could be of help to the pioneers of exploration and of war, of technology and all the forces that were at work remaking the face of the earth. The 'New World' was christianized thanks to this conquest; what is more, it became a christianizing force, though not without paying the price of Puritan hypocrisy. Without too much demur Protestantism accepted that bourgeois failure which conceals a lax or primitive morality behind a show of strictness; it was willing to bring the Bible and the canons at the same time. Spanish Catholicism had done the same, of course, and with greater cruelty. It had had its Inquisition, but it did not have its puritanism. Its masks have always been more visible, avowed more openly, and consequently more readily disavowed.

The contraries of every age bear a certain resemblance to each other. It might be claimed that the methods of the Jesuits were at bottom analogous to those of Calvin. St Ignatius' disciples, too, preserve an ark, an island, an inviolate enclave: the faith of Rome, subordination to the Pope, strict obedience to their general, the trained discipline of their whole being. Assured, re-assured by these areas of radical purity and integrity, the Jesuits were wholly free to carry adaptation to the new and modern world as far as it would go, free *to love the world* and be forebearing toward any customs of the world that were not radically evil. Leibniz was in the same position: beneath his calculator God, that unique Monad removed even from the will to choose, Leibniz could *organize the earth*, rejecting nothing and improving everything there was.

Be that as it may, we note that the Reformers—like the Arians, Montanists, Catharists—meant to restore the *purity* of the early Church. In a religion of revelation and tradition such as the religion of Abraham and Jesus, perfection stands at the beginning; purification often appears as a revival of the beginning. At first this was the whole subject of the controversy. The Protestants claimed that they were keeping to Scripture only, and returning to the practices of the early Church. They reproached the Catholics for their innovations, such as the veneration of saints, for example, or communion under the single species of the bread. In his reply to the Protestant pastors Bossuet, though vigorously asserting the inflexibility of the Roman position, defended a certain variation of discipline. In later days, Protestant thinkers would take pride in having introduced diversity and in having made changes. The Reformation, more so perhaps than any other Western religious movement, had no intention to conserve an unadulterated past. It soon laid claim to a spirit of freedom, variety, variation, even of evolution; and so it paved the way for the modern spirit which is so receptive to progress and mutation. If the basis of faith lies in that I listen within myself to the free Word spoken to the free conscience, then clearly the rules of an ancient and often imprecise Scripture may be interpreted in very many ways, according to personalities or groups.

Catholics, then as now, have found it difficult to understand how the Protestants who came after sixteen centuries of ecclesiastical tradition could be so sure that they were transmitting Christ's revelation. And they are grateful when Reformed exegetes and theologians, faithful to history, recognize that Scripture was created, collected, and canonised by the Church which is anterior to Scripture.

In fact, this collection of the signs which Christ left behind has been collected, put together, established, preserved, and equipped with commentary by the Church that was being born:

The Protestant Reformation

the Church of the apostles, and of their successors the bishops. This preservation and textual explication, which was a constant process among the Jewish people where prophet interpreted prophet, is being continued in the Catholic Church. Protestants maintain, however, that Scripture remains the *only* rule of faith. To them it seems clear and decisive. Catholics believe that any Writ, however divine, contains seeds that develop, gaps that close, and ambiguities that are cleared up through history.

Catholics are troubled to see that the faith of their brothers brings with it so many differences and divergences in time and space. They anxiously ask their brothers to help them understand how the Spirit of truth, which must be one, faithful, and consistent, does, in fact, for three centuries now supply the intellectuals and theologians of the Reform with answers that at times are so contradictory.

To this question, our brothers reply at times that the Catholic mind exaggerates the importance of these differences, and that the same differences exist, less visible, within the highly disciplined Church of Rome. More importantly and more profoundly, they tell us that the Catholic mind does not have easy access to what constitutes the powerful, radical, and tormented originality of Protestantism. This originality is not limited to reclaiming the freedom of the believer; it is not limited to a recourse to Scripture alone, and still less to the rejection of Catholicism, its practices and customs: all this is incidental. The essence is hidden more deeply—and the essence is what needs to be understood.

What is the essence of Protestantism?

Beyond all the different forms of Protestantism over which its enemies rejoice, beyond even the customs and attitudes of soul which are common throughout the Protestant world (but which might have been different if Protestantism had not arisen out of a protest) there is something invariable, an essence of thought and of faith which, so to speak, is supra-historical and timeless; which under a different set of circumstances could have appeared at the very beginning, immediately after the apostolic age, when the bishops assumed the place left vacant by the Apostles.

The problem with which the intellect of our time must deal, therefore, is to determine whether the rise of Protestantism in the world is narrowly dependent upon that combination of circumstances which occurred in the sixteenth century, or whether Protestantism contains a principle which is independent of that historical accident.

In the first case, the Reformation would be no more than a passing interlude, which would lose its validity as soon as the abuses it opposed had fully disappeared. In the second case, the Reformation would be as alive as it was on the day when it first emerged into history, and perhaps even more fully alive because it has grown in self-awareness. And if so, then traces of it should virtually be discoverable in earlier epochs, *when it was always on the point of emerging*; back even to the origins of Christianity, to Christ himself whose true message it would in this case represent.

Such is the conviction of the present-day *thinkers* of Protestantism, whether their name be Karl Barth or Paul Tillich. In two different contexts, one German, the other American, they tend to distinguish the Reformation of history from a Reformation that is much deeper and more permanent. Behind the great Reformers of dogma they seek to define a principle which is superior to their assertions, and which would be truly the principle itself, the *essence of Protestantism* by which Protestantism is opposed to Catholicism.

For Tillich, whose influence in America is growing, the religious depth of our age is not expressed in the Churches; it finds expression rather in cultural movements such as the sciences, the philosophies, the arts, politics. Twentieth century mankind is searching for a religion at once old and new, which beyond the religious institutions could achieve the synthesis of all aspirations, as Christianity did in the first centuries. This religion would be Protestantism, provided it were truly pure and confined to its principle: the denial of every human, concrete, conceptual means of union with the Being, the Beyond, the Altogether Other.

In spite of considerable differences Karl Barth and Tillich are not in total opposition. And their resemblance at the core is, I believe, the point where we must look for the axiom which is presupposed prior to all else in their thought system, the axiom in which the real choice is made.

I shall try, then, to throw light upon that point, even at the risk that the light may be blinding. It can always be dimmed. I would say that the essence of any thought system of a Protestant type must be sought in the postulate, more philosophical almost than it is theological, that a choice must be made between God and man, between faith and 'works', between grace and freedom, between justification and sanctification . . . in such a fashion that if God acts in us, man can in no way act himself. A choice must be made in such a fashion that any assent to a pair of complementaries—God and Man, faith and reason, visible and invisible priesthood—is in practice unthinkable. By logical deduction, then, every spiritual exercise, every work of proof and reason, all priestly mediation, all intercession in prayer, all real merit—in short, every interval, every intermediary between the nothingness of the sinner and the Divine Infinity, is suspect. At its worst it must be condemned as contrary to the Spirit, whom Christ has brought, and whom St Paul has defined so brilliantly especially in Romans. If that is so, then the Reformation did not begin in the sixteenth century. The sixteenth century, and perhaps even more the twentieth, are periods of volcanic eruption and emergence. But the principle which justifies the separation from the Church of Rome is co-extensive in time with that Church, and goes back to the gospel.

As I study and compare the most eminent thinkers of Protestantism today—for example, Karl Barth, Oscar Cullmann, or Bultmann, the masters of dogmatics, history of salvation, and exegesis—however much they may differ among themselves, I yet gain from them the same impression of a timeless essence, of the 'perennial nature' of Protestantism as a primal choice.

Both the logic of theology, and the critical study of the texts and of history, appear to the Protestant thinkers to agree in showing that the Catholic error began very early. Renan placed it within the historical life of Jesus, when Jesus, in letting himself be baptized by the Judaic John, seemed to break faith with his original conception of an ideal religion without ritual. Harnack saw the moment of rupture in the misunderstanding between Jesus and his Apostles, who supposedly mistook the Master's intentions. Goguel, Cullmann, and Karl Barth place the break between the Church of the Apostles, which continues Jesus, and the Church of 'the successors of the Apostles', that is, the bishops who are already paleocatholics, the apostolic fathers, who are already catholicizing. This would imply that Christ after his dismemberment on the cross, has been in agony in His Church from the beginning.

Let us add at once that according to several interpreters the rupture, though it occurred almost at the beginning, was due not so much to a fault, a breach of the faith, as to the bondage of existence whereby no civilization can be pure: *the Kingdom is never of this world*. As for the rest, the embers of the saints have never stopped glowing to many Protestants, and go on giving heat from beneath the Roman ashes. This truly Christian Christianity had been practised among the best for sixteen hundred years before the *awakening* of the Reformation; it is the ground on which rests the faith of the Saints, the great doctors, the true Catholic mystics, such as St Augustine, St Bernard, St Francis of Assisi, and so many others. These pure men have in effect been animated by that same spirit which the Fathers of the Reformation, men of lesser virtue, defined with such violence.

I said that all 'great heresies' spoke the same language. Not one of them intended innovation. They all thought of themselves as a return to a primal purity that was not altogether lost but had been compromised everywhere except among the elect. This heroic love of integrity allowed them to face without trembling their rejection by the visible unity in order that they might save the invisible unity; once the separation had been consummated, they could find in it a somber and severe glory.

The definition I just proposed risks being too abstract, empty of inner life. I meant to show in what way these principles nourish the life of conscience. There is no testimony more lucid than that of Mlle C. de Vogel. It will be objected that Mlle de Vogel, later a convert to Catholicism, is not a reliable witness. But to convert does not mean to deny oneself. I believe that only those who have lived vigorously and arduously in these two universes of faith that divide us have experienced the difference to the full, and may help us to overcome it.

In 1933, Mlle de Vogel made a study of the conversion of

Ernest Psichari, the grandson of Renan. Psichari had become a Christian, she said, because in the end he recognized in Jesus Christ the son of God. But 'he became a Catholic because he stopped too soon, thinking that he had found the absolute in an institutional Church, as though the Absolute could ever be tangible in this world. The Absolute has become manifest among us only once—in the Christ himself; and it remains in Him, but in Heaven and not on earth, at least not in the direct meaning of those who put in its place a concrete ecclesiastical organization. Had Psichari gone further, to greater depths, he would have become a Protestant and not a Catholic'.

The author next tries to discover the 'essence' of Protestantism and, to begin with, its external aspects. Our author states that this essence seems to her to reside in a simple and direct view of the gospel. This spiritual perspective, which the Protestant believer finds unvaryingly confirmed in the Bible, constitutes for her an integral unity; no part of this biblical vision of things must be relinquished, and nothing alien could be added to it. Either would be a mutilation and falsification of the gospel.

The believer is fully aware that to his left and to his right there are other communities which also claim the name of Jesus Christ for themselves: on one side liberal Protestantism, on the other Roman Catholicism. Liberal Protestantism cannot be the Church for him, because it does not understand the true Gospel, the Gospel of the Incarnation and of reconciliation by the Cross. He could go into a Dutch Reformed Church, or into a Church that came out of the first or the second dissidence, or again into a Lutheran Church—it does not matter so long as he hears there the proclamation that God, taking on a human body, has come among us to bring salvation to us mortals. But he could not go any place where this combination is neither understood nor believed. For there the Church is not.

What happens, one is curious to know, when he goes into a Roman Church? Let us hear Mlle de Vogel. She will surprise us:

'There, he hears no proclamation of the Word Incarnate, the Lamb that has taken away our sins. At the center here, there is a rite in the course of which one pretends that Jesus Christ, on a word spoken by the priest, becomes bodily present on the altar.

Before this miracle, one bows down to worship. Our Protestant believer has learned from his youth on up to consider this rank superstition. And what else could it be? To materialize in this way the spiritual realities that we are given to believe—is that not to debase and falsify the very Gospel?

'We are told also how much there is in the cult of the Roman Church that is impressive: the beauties of her buildings, of the form and vestments of her liturgy, and of Gregorian chant. True, all of this may be beautiful to the eye and to the ear. But what does it mean to our souls, if the content is not *true*? Thus, after all, we are not impressed. On the contrary.

'The same goes for the much vaunted unity of Catholicism. Unity is assuredly an evangelical attribute of the true Church. Must we not then admire and envy this unity of the Catholic Church which alone realizes what Protestant Christianity, with all its good intentions and attempts, has to admit as lying beyond its reach? No, once again, we cannot admire that unity, because at bottom it rests upon falsehood. We desire the unity of the Church—but never at that price, never at the expense of truth. That is why we neither admire nor envy Roman unity, however beautiful it may appear from the outside. More beautiful to us, because more authentic, is the unity in faith of our own Protestant Church, seemingly so divided.

'With us, consequently, there is outward multiplicity but inward unity, founded in Him who gave to us the gift of faith, He of Whom we are the members. And the Roman Church, outwardly a unity, does she not have her theological disagreements? Certainly. However, there is a fundamental unity of faith—a unity which allows, of course, for a measure of theological elaboration, but which no theologian could question within the framework of the Church. For there exists a central authority which in the name of Christ exacts absolute submission: a *human* authority, which has claimed for itself infallibility.

'Here we are face to face with a materialization analogous to that which occurred at the Holy Supper: the Absolute is once more linked to a finite and ephemeral form . . .

'This attitude of the Protestant Christian is often very poorly understood on the Catholic side. It is thought that the characteristic trait of the Protestant attitude is negation. Now the

Protestant Christian is an evangelical Christian. His faith is strong and positive. If he has had to protest, it is because of historical circumstances: the blame for it must be placed not upon him but on the Roman Church which separated herself from her origins. Before God and his conscience, the Protestant knows that in order to hold firmly to the Word revealed by God he must take this position which, seen from the other side, has the odious character of a schism.

'He cannot do otherwise. His protest against Rome is identical with his fidelity to the Lord.'

Finally, our author asks herself how such an attitude could be shaken. She says:

'It would be necessary to make us understand one way or the other that the intention of Jesus Christ was not what we have so far thought it was; that He has "founded" a Church in a more concrete sense; that He has given Himself to us in the Sacrament in a more concrete fashion; that He lends to His Church a more direct assistance, and that the history of the Church, studied more closely, does not bear the aspect we have assumed. Then, and only then, would we recognize—not without pain nor extreme difficulty—that what the Reformation has opposed to the Roman Church is not the pure Gospel of Jesus Christ and his Apostles but, putting the matter in the most favorable terms, a partial and hence still disfigured Gospel. Only then should we be able to revise profoundly our ideas about the Church and Christianity—only then—but, then, obedience to the Christ may force us finally to leave the place which is now ours: the Church where the sacred names of the Father, the Son, and the Spirit have been spoken over us, the place which because of Christ was dearer to us than anything in the world.'

The Catholics who think that they can trouble Protestant consciences by alerting them to the faults of the Fathers of the Reformation rejoice too soon. A Protestant soul imbued with the idea of original sin is not swayed by the sanctity of a sinner any more easily than it is surprised at the fall of a just man. Protestants do not think that the Church must *visibly* be one and holy. Their Church often glories in its infirmity rather than cover it up. She is not startled to see living within her liberals whom the freedom of interpretation leads toward critical doubt and religious rationalism, side by side with dogmatic minds who confess strictly the original faith of Luther and of Calvin. There are distinct levels in every conscience, and at times we admit on one level what we reject on another. But it may generally be said that Protestant spirituality is more tolerant of contradictions than Catholic spirituality—as may be seen by a comparison of Descartes, Pascal, Malebranche, Catholic thinkers, with Leibniz, Kant, and Hegel, Protestant thinkers. A Protestant intelligence can hold within itself, side by side and in all loyalty, both the faith in Christ's resurrection and the denial of his historicity. Goguel and Bultmann feel no embarrassment in admitting that in the eyes of science Jesus is dead and the belief in his resurrection is based on hallucinations—this does not keep them from 'believing in the resurrection'. This opposition of certitudes, now, this partition of conscience, this co-existence of *homo peccator* and *homo justus*, of man seen from the point of view of science and man seen from the point of view of faith, is the normal condition of created, fallen, and redeemed man. One might even say that an incurable inner rift is the sign of predestination, a necessary condition for a certain spiritual health. There must be torment at the heart of true peace. Modern man has in many ways laicized these concepts.

A Catholic who studies the motivating causes of the Protestant Reformation may ask himself, as I said, whether they are still fully valid. He notes that for some decades now, there are fewer disagreements between theologians and intellectuals. Both sides admit Scripture, the creeds and symbols of the Faith, the mystery of the Incarnation, even the principal sacraments. Just a little bit of good will, it seems, would be enough to bring about a meeting. Theologians and scholars have studied the diverse intellectual currents in the medieval Church and shown that certain Catholics in the Augustinian tradition who are considered orthodox, and even Thomism, have expressed views on original sin, and the justification by faith, which are not so different from the Protestant position. The canons and anathemas of the Second Council of Orange against the Semi-Pelagians seems very close to the formulations of the Reformation. A reader of Karl Barth comes away with the impression of a tragic misunderstanding due to language, concepts, habits, due to the way in which we think our feelings and feel our thoughts, rather than to a difference in substance.

Henceforth we may ask ourselves whether the dismemberment of Christianity caused by the initiative of the Reformers is not on the wane.

There is no decline in numbers. Protestant reality is a considerable reality. Two hundred and eighty million Christian souls have their roots in the Reformation. Great nations are imbued with it. The Protestant Churches are suffering, of course, from the growth of indifference, as are all religions. If we recall the triumphant position Protestantism held in the middle of the last century, especially politically and intellectually, we cannot fail to see that it shows signs of decline, especially as regards real piety among its faithful and the faith of its élite. Catholicism suffers the same afflictions, but resists more effectively because of its coherence.

In the present chapter I have raised the difficult but most important question about the real motives of faith. Can it be held that the assent of the believers springs from the same causes at this present hour as it did in the days when Protestantism originated in the sixteenth century? And what was then the principal and driving motive that made so large a multitude of men reject the traditional religion of their fathers? The Catholic who became a convert to the Reformed religion did not act because he had difficulties with *faith* or *grace*—he neither did nor could understand them. He followed a general movement; he obeyed his prince and his natural leaders. He was supported by the feeling that the Church he saw before him needed reforming. The new religion, unburdened in its cult, more biblical and more *Paulinian* (I do not say more *evangelical*) gave greater scope to the laity, used a more intelligible language, and so met much better the needs of certain religious temperaments. Then came history, and chasms opened between the consciences. Habits took root. And there was no more dialogue on any level.

If the Christians of the twentieth century were now one single Catholic community, two hundred and eighty millions of them would not secede today in order to adopt the religion of Luther and Calvin. In other words, the effective Protestant faith of the masses is not concerned *with what separates* the Protestant from the Catholic doctrine, but rather with what they hold in common. Converts from Protestantism to Catholicism, such as Newman or in our own day Mlle de Vogel and Bouyer, testify that when they became Catholic they did not feel they were denying their Protestant faith, but rather that they were fulfilling it.

In the last twenty years we have witnessed the growth within Protestantism of a strong ecumenical movement. Does it intend to reform the Reform? Or to sublimate it? These questions are being asked in several quarters.

It has been asked why Protestantism was not missionary in its early days. Was it because the idea of predestination is contrary to the idea of mission? If God has already chosen his elect, then why gratuitously proclaim the gospel to them? However, the function of the apostle's preaching is just this, to make the name and face of the elect stand out. It has been said also that the Reformation proclaimed the gospel more as God's word to the Church in her full power than as the word which God speaks to the world at large in order to convert it. The *kerygma*, however, combines these two voices. It has been said that in the eyes of the Reformers the missionary apostolate was a privilege which belonged to the apostles and was not transferable—yet one can transmit part of one's belongings. It has been said that God would save his elect without intermediaries, and that those who, yielding to misplaced compassion, went out on missions were trying to usurp part of God's judgment, using as their pretext the ignorance of nations deprived of the insights of the gospel. It has been said that the Protestants, in answer to their critics in the Roman Church, demonstrated the indivisibility of the Church by renouncing that visibility which a missionary movement would have secured for their Church. It has been said that it was distaste for missionary religious orders which prompted them not to undertake such things.

Be that as it may, Protestant Church missions were set up on the fringes of the established Church, at times in an open break with the official Church; they were set up by small societies, on the inspiration of some mystic, somewhat in the way in which colonization was started and developed by pioneers who were not too well regarded by the metropolitan authorities, the way in which France found herself with an Empire without having much wanted it. Thus the world of the Reformation took pleasure in this half-unwanted child, its missionary drive which was so ardent and efficacious. As the nations of Europe gloried in the colonial empires brought to them by their prodigal children, so the Protestant Churches came to understand that the mission of Christ in the world of the pagans was their most worthy outward fruit.

The mission, now, was powerful in its ecumenism. In fact, confessional distinctions which set the various spiritual families against each other had to be passed over in silence when dealing with the pagans. How could one present a religion of unity and love, all gathered round the faith in Jesus Christ, if that religion is cut up into societies with different formularies and rites, some having bishops like the Lutherans and Anglicans, while others only had a presbytery? The Catholics are not familiar with these difficulties because the liturgy of their Latin mass is the same in all climates.

This necessity of a re-grouping compels Protestantism to return to its sources. It must return to its profoundest idea, its first well-spring, which is to bear witness to Christ. Without ceasing to be itself, Protestantism is in a new way growing aware of its unity. In the past it has found such unity in its dogma of *Faith* and *Grace*, that is, in a purely theological manner which is the manner least likely to call forth zeal. Henceforth, unity is experienced in the convergence toward an apostolic goal: the point at stake is to make certain that atheism does not overtake peoples that have not yet been touched by the gospel message. The point at stake is to save the spiritual world from a death still more radical than the death which threatened it in the time of Jesus; for then paganism had faith in the divinity, and felt respect for the rôle of mystery. The point is to lend to the Protestant message all of its power to save and to open up—if I may use a Bergsonian idea, to make Protestantism pass from incompleteness to completeness, from the *closed* to the *open*.

In fact, Protestantism was originally not truly open and universal, even though it wanted to be. Lutheranism was Germanic. Protestant societies conformed to national boundaries —they were following the pattern of the large political bodies.

But thanks to the opening up of the missionary movement, the idea of a unity *to come* will from now on lend greater richness to the idea of the unity *of the past*, faithful to Luther and his interpretation of St Augustine and St Paul. Thus the deepest intention of the Protestant world is being insensibly transformed. The relations among the various Reformed communities are modified. Though they remain different, they henceforth have an organ to make them aware of their mutual contributions to the evangelization of the world.

The same transformation of attitude and of communication is noticeable also in the relations between Protestants and Catholics. Ever since the Reformation, the two communities have been compelled in certain countries to find their places side by side, like pieces in a jig-saw puzzle. Though they no longer make war on each other, though they avoid polemics, they think of one another constantly. The Protestant community does the larger share of the thinking, in keeping with the fact that it has grown out of a protest. If there were no Catholicism in the world, Protestantism would be altogether different, and its cohesion would, no doubt, be quite other, and less solid.

Some observers are pessimistic. Their views come down to something like this: 'The two communions suffer from the rift. Because they are living face to face and are under each other's influence, they have emphasized the line of difference. It has become clear that short of a last-minute miracle they will not visibly join each other.' So far no division among Christians has ever been repaired. I once heard Lord Halifax quoting a poet: 'They parted never to meet again.' As time goes on, beliefs sink their roots more firmly into custom and continuity; they become loyalties and points of honor; a simple *colloquy* cannot be expected to bring about reunion.

A premature reunion might even be something to be feared. For the Roman Church must be ready to receive, the others must be ready to come. Neither is possible without a painful inner travail on both sides, a deep searching of souls and sensibilities, even when dogmatic obstacles are removed.

But in these problems which border on the insoluble, and in an extraordinary period like our own, I find it difficult to say:

that will never happen. The word impossible has never been in the Divine language: it is ruled out by hope.

Beyond the relations of return or condemnation, a relation of convergence and of harmony is taking shape which stems from the deepening of the idea of mission, caused by the pressure to make common front against a danger that would indiscriminately and without distinction undermine all Christendom. I mentioned the scandal caused among non-Christians by the diversity of forms of Protestantism. Another shock is the implacable division between Christians according to their membership either in the Catholic Church or in the other Christian Churches. To an outsider, an unbeliever who is tempted to believe, the opposition between Catholic mission and Protestant mission demonstrates the Christians' inability to practise the love they preach. The Holy Spirit urges both sides to put a stop to this cleavage, or at least to reduce it to a point where it is no longer an obstacle to evangelization.

This need for unity, or at least for an effacement and forgetfulness of disunity, should give rise to a growing *spirit of charity in truth*—or, to use the new word needed here, *ecumenism.* We note in passing that this Greek word, meaning 'the whole inhabited earth as if it were a common home' (*oikos*), expresses the same desire as the old Greek word 'catholic', meaning 'over the whole extent'. Ecumenism contains the idea of a gathering together, of effective and world-wide communion. At a minimum, it means that 'humanity' stops being merely a word, that Christianity would be re-born.

However: as long as Christians are divided on the one hand into a Church which admits no other unity than within herself, and on the other, Churches which are willing to unite among themselves despite dogmatic conflicts; in other words, as long as Christians are divided between the ideal of Unity and the ideal of Union, ideals that are in reality incompatible and in some ways conflicting; just so long, there must necessarily, logically, and in terms of Christianity be not one ecumenism, but two.

We could conceive of a single, vast and comprehensive ecumenism that would gather together Catholics and non-Catholics under the same ideal of desire. It would proceed by definitions of the minimum granted by either side, and by preliminary propositions. Such an ecumenism can exist in virtue of mystic hope, and in the intentions of prayer. It might produce balanced, intentionally imprecise formulations. There is sometimes a useful art of ecumenism which consists in not defining. But once we leave this preserve of the specialists, sages, or mystics, a single ecumenism will necessarily be a mongrel breed. It sets opposing beliefs on the same level; it lends currency to the false notion that they are in agreement, and the still falser notion that they are two different expressions of a truth which is superior to both of them. But no true believer of any confession will accept such an abdication of faith. Protestants and Catholics remain separated because they both are certain that they hold the truth, and that their distant brothers ought to convert in order to be faithful to Christ. Both prefer separation to the false union of compromise, as one would prefer suffering to lying.[1]

A secret logic here guides history. What was it that we have witnessed between 1961 and 1963? Two meetings, one at Delhi, and one of the Vatican Council. There is a Protestant ecumenism, or rather a non-Catholic—and that does not mean anti-Catholic —ecumenism which brings together the Churches that are outside the unity of Rome, and strives to awaken or to make explicit among them their underlying unity in the Christ Jesus. And the Roman Church, too, which cannot without self-negation renounce her claim to be the *only* Church, has its Catholic ecumenism. It is above all else an effort to discern what the Church of the twentieth century—after so long a past, so many losses and rifts—must specify, correct, renew, and develop in order to make possible a common life with the at last reunited Christians.

[1]Professor Cullmann, for his part, expressed himself as follows: 'What keeps the Protestants from a return to Rome is, we must realize, the very concept of the Church, of infallibility and of unity. In the same way it is our conception of the Church and her unity that keeps the Catholic Church from recognizing the Protestant Churches as legitimate Churches. At most, the Catholic Church can recognize among us "Church vestiges".

'This painful situation must be faced. There is no use having illusions. As far as can humanly be foreseen, the *unity* of the Church, as between Protestants and Catholics, is no longer possible—not unless the Catholics accept the Protestant conception or the Protestants accept the Catholic conception. But that would simply mean the disappearance of one or the other, and so has nothing to do with our problem.'

These two ecumenisms are converging toward the same goal, complete fidelity to Christ.

If these convergences were to run their full course, if these converging lines were to vanish at their apex, there would be a problem no longer. We may not hope for that short of a *metastrophe* impossible to foresee. And it may be God's will for the Christians to keep these communities in this yearning and prayer for unity, in this intention to draw close to each other.

There may, in fact, be beneath the divisions loyalties that remain unexpressed, desires that are impossible to satisfy, and words impossible to utter. Catholic theologians of all times have charted the map of this realm of sanctity, which extends beyond the visible frontiers of the Church, and which has at times been called 'the soul of the Church'. St Augustine let it be understood that 'the body' and 'the soul' do not coincide—that the Church has children among her enemies, and enemies among her children. Today perhaps more than ever, psychoanalytic inquiry draws our attention to virtualities, unconscious notions, the hidden part of the mind. In the unconscious minds of the baptized there is clearly a greater desire than ever for visible communion across the frontiers of dogma. The ecclesiastical hierarchy of the two communities is bound to react against this tendency, which would end up in brotherly confusion. The suffering that men have shared—for instance in concentration camps or in underground work—the feeling of a common danger and also, let us admit, a decline of faith due to lay education and the loss of the sense of mystery, all these have encouraged a tendency toward vague assimilation. This is the context which allows us to realize fully how salutary is this *dyad* of ecumenisms; for it prevents the sincere but clumsy good-will of the faithful from producing a Christianity of the gnostic type that is made up of vague syntheses. To a religion, a synthesis of that kind is merely the beginning of the end.

Protestantism is the most important religious fact of the last three hundred years, not so much because of the doctrine itself, as I have said, as because of the success of that doctrine, and of the theologico-political phenomenon it represents. Are we to say that Protestantism, like other 'great decisions' before it in history, has lasted for practically three hundred years—and therefore will maintain itself from now on, though without further growth? Or is it on the contrary the religion of the future?

Toward the end of the nineteenth century one might have thought so. Bergson has stated that this was what he then believed. But today, the matter is once again problematical. The religion of the future will either be an irreligion enforced by the state and its propaganda; or else it will be a 'rejuvenated' Catholicism such as John XXIII and his successor desire, identical with itself, constructive, and recapitulatory.

From the Catholic point of view, which I myself have taken in this book, one would hope that the Protestant faith might develop in a more positive rather than negative and protesting manner. If the idea which Protestant theologians and Protestant believers have of Catholicism is not always just, as we think, if they see the outward appearance rather than the inner truth, then it is up to us Catholics to reduce that astounding divergence between being and appearance by sharper definitions and greater authenticity. If there is at a greater depth such an abysmal difference concerning the essence of Christianity as I have said, then it is up to both of us, Catholics and Protestants joined around the same table, to discover together, by an effort that involves our whole being and all of our knowledge, the way of God's will. And if after that dialogue there is left an unbridgeable difference, let its solution be entrusted to the depth of the secret of God. And let us pursue our roads, the one and the other, in sorrow at the rift but from now on in love, and in hope.

A last question remains in every ecumenical mind that believes in the visible Church: how to conceive the regrouping of the Churches? Unity can practically be formed only around the Roman Church. That Church is blamed for not being the center, axis, focus, meeting place—but instead, of making unity dependent on conditions that seem incompatible with the faith, the ancient rules, and the legitimate independence of the communities. From the separated Churches we hear the lover's plaint: '*Nec tecum nec sine te vivere possum*—I can do nothing with you. I can do nothing without you.' The charge that nothing can be done with the Catholic Church has been made often enough, by accusations, criticism, or by silences; and by the old separation itself which finds a double confirmation in that it continues, and that there is no doubt of its justice. But the very existence of those ecumenical sessions, in the secret desire for a presence they know to be impossible, gives tacit recognition also to the fact that without the Roman focus an effective unity can never be reached.

There emerges from all this the idea, almost impossible to put in words, of a reaching forward to a future stage of the Roman Church, as yet impossible to define, when the Roman Church would really be the center of re-assembly for all Christians, which would allow them to achieve their vocation *without having to strip off their garment, but putting on another garment, so that what is mortal in them may be steeped in life: the Father's house with many mansions.*

When will it be?

The New Dismemberment

I NOW TURN TO OUR OWN TIME. IT BELONGS PARTLY TO the past and partly to the future. It resembles a wave the moment before it breaks. Hence the tentative nature of my remarks.

There are many signs that the era whose upheavals we have surveyed peak by peak has reached a turning point, and that religious revolutions from now on will take a different form. We may still expect, no doubt, that national Churches will be split off under pressure from the political powers; schisms of that kind, even large schisms, may still be expected. But those events will be without theological significance: they will not issue in dogmatic quarrels about the divinity of Christ, or the relation between 'justification' and 'sanctification', or the merit of the sacraments. The reason is that 'heresy', religious quarrels, and division among Christians presuppose an underlying faith held in common. Opponents in the faith necessarily share a large foundation of absolute agreement. However, the characteristic mark of the epoch through which we are advancing now, and into which we have imperceptibly been moving for the last three hundred years, is that the faith is growing cold. There is today not enough religion left on earth to give rise to an explicitly religious heresy. One might think the end of the world is close at hand, if we are to attach a specific meaning to the moan of Jesus: 'When the Son of Man returns, will he still find faith on earth?'

The First Vatican Council could find no truly religious heresies that called for condemnation, but only philosophies that were a danger to right reason. Not that the faith was stronger; rather, the enemy made his attack at a deeper level; his charges, or rather his sapping tunnels, are undermining the substructures, the natural foundations that were once mankind's common heritage.

The new age shows an attenuation of the faith at least in its visible and established forms. In contrast to preceding ages we witness today the weakening if not the end of that state of affairs when religion was upheld by an institution or an environment other than itself; by political power, for example, or social structure, custom, usage, language, sensibility, or atmosphere.

It is not easy to tell to what extent faith has disappeared; we cannot readily determine how far the faith of preceding ages, when it coincided with institution, was a true personal adherence or mere conformism. We shall never know. It is useless to ask ourselves these questions without answers: not even the men of the preceding ages whom we would have questioned could have given the answer. When a whole world thinks alike, non-conformism remains unspoken.

Since the Renaissance the separation between the universe of man and the universe of the Christian is becoming visible. Ever since mankind has become conscious of itself it has had this idea of its unity. The ancient myths gave it the feeling of unity: polytheistic when it came to gods, mankind was monanthropic for itself. Though there were many gods there was only one human race, and only one first man. But the notion of 'barbaric' nations, the impossibility of matching the various chronologies, ignorance of the origins and uncertainty about the end, the lack of the idea of progress, the myth of the 'eternal return'—all these made it difficult for total man to know himself. The Church made that knowledge possible for him: and for a long time it was one and the same thing for man to think of himself as man, and to think of himself as a Christian, a member of the Christian Church.

Today, by contrast, there is so vast a contradiction between the two points of view that it is difficult, and to some of us impossible, to think of ourselves as men and as Christians *at the same time*. This opposition always existed, but modern man has carried the division of the two forms of being to extremes. The forms are 'concordant'. However, concordance, concordate, and concord are ambiguous words. They dispose of the suspicion, of course, that there is too visible a rivalry; but for all that they do not mean that there is harmony, mutual understanding, or accord. Power frequently tries only to smother as far as possible those religions which it no longer persecutes simply because it prefers to ignore them.

Heresy, being a difference in faiths, presupposes an ardent faith to which the difference in beliefs—even of an *iota*—is so important that everything must be done to maintain it, including a break of the bonds of union and the appeal to temporal powers for help. And usually it is possible to find a power willing to persecute you, or to help you persecute.

Jung holds that behind every *iota* there is the great psychological schism: 'On the one side there is the assertion that the important, essential world is that which is perceived by the senses . . . On the other side there is the assertion that the essential resides outside of the human.' The same *iota*, it would seem, has separated religion and rationalism. It is the same problem, always and everywhere.

We may look forward to a weakening of the Christian Churches which are supported by a state or an empire. The state no longer needs them, and will no longer take the trouble of seeming to believe in them. The 'prince' in the flannel suit will no longer be tempted, as was Henry VIII, to be another Charlemagne.

The choice with which the common man is faced, therefore, is no longer one between several forms of Christianity, but between two world views of which one believes in Transcendence while the other denies it. Within the first of the two alternatives, several choices can, of course, be made, but they are apparently secondary. We do not find today men tearing each other apart over the meaning of grace; but they kill each other over the problem of knowing whether the first thing is Nothingness.

How are we to know that this is not the choice that was concealed in the depths of the great options of the past, that those options were not in reality concerned with Transcendence? How do we know that Arius, when he reduced Christ to his temporal aspect, which compared with eternity is Nothing, did not in fact choose Nothingness? Who can tell whether certain current forms of the existentialist or the Marxist Denial will not bring back a theology of immanence? Or whether the revolts and revolutions in the name of purity which are today so frequent are not simply new versions of the Catharist protest? Or that there is not brewing in the darkness of our time a new mixture of the Arian type between imperialism and Christianity? Or that a new gnosticism would not be successful? Or that a new Islam might not arise? The number of themes is small, and time is long.

We are witnesses to a phenemonon which is analogous, though

in reverse, to the rise of Christianity. A *tertium genus humanum*, a third species of man, is slipping quietly into the substructures of this world, just as the *tertium genus christianorum* slipped into the Roman Empire during its time of decadence. The man who holds no faith—not because he is ignorant, but because he believes to have outgrown belief—feels as much contempt for the Christian faith as the first Christians felt for paganism. To the new man, it is Christianity that seems the *myth*. He is mistaken. For he imagines that science, history, criticism have cast Jesus back into the realm of legend together with all the mythologies. In fact, true science and true criticism have reinforced the reasons for believing in the substance of the gospel.

Since the beginnings of mankind we have seen more than once the appearance of a new race of men who seemed to have no standard in common with those who occupied the land before them. Relations between the old and the new race take the form of warfare, or at least incomprehension. *Homo judaicus* and *homo christianus* were such *neo-anthropoi*. Marxist man, again, would seem to be a *neo-anthropos*.

Even in Christian societies there have been 'libertins', who did not accept the common rules of faith or of reason. Deep-searching thinkers, among them Pascal, Leibniz, Newman, and Dostoevski, have foreseen the coming of this separation between the two universes of thought. They tried to throw a foot-bridge over the abyss by mean of 'apologetics', which are techniques to reduce differences.

But, as Newman has seen, the new man does not confront Christianity in the way the barbarians did, who were ignorant and felt inferior and left behind. The new man thinks that he has been evangelized and has refuted the Evangel. He has become immune to the bad news, the Christian 'disease'. Here lies the main difficulty, which changes all aspects of the problem: there is no precedent to which to turn.

Toward the end of the Roman Empire, the Christians had been living in poverty, insecurity, concealment—without position, without power, and even without tradition, since the Jewish tradition was unknown to those converts that had been gentiles. They were living outside of social time, with martydom hanging over their heads at any moment. But no sooner did they get power, civilization, and the responsibility for the human tradition than they created a 'Christian order'. Instead of cutting themselves off from their time, and thinking of themselves as stowaways on a ship that is bound to founder, they put their hands to the tasks that their time called for. They were now in possession, though Christ had been dispossessed.

Today for the first time in history the mystique of dispossession is being used against the Christians. The Marxist argument relies upon the demonstration that Christianity and possession are inextricably intermixed. I use the term 'possession' in its broad meaning of having charge—charge of culture, or charge of the past and of history: *onus, honor.*

Understandably, this misunderstanding can rise to the point of paroxysm. The Christian looks at his enemy, but he can neither classify nor understand him: the enemy does not play by the rules, he inhabits a country not charted on any map.

From the eighteenth century onward, there have been men who have accepted a progressive time, in contrast with the ecclesiastical time whose function is conservation and constant mending to counter-balance decay. The 'philosophers' asserted that mankind was growing ever more perfect from age to age; complete perfection would come at the end—and that end was near. The messianic time of the Jews, from which we draw the comfort of a hope that cannot be disappointed, here re-appeared in secular guise. Awareness of the progress made so far keeps our faith strong and fresh: we need go on only a little longer. The words of the gospel, *only a little while*, these words of a living hope are handed on forever.

I am writing these thoughts during a moment of suspense, in the interval between sessions of the Vatican Council. Like Job I here must raise a finger to my lips. Nothing is more impenetrable and obscure to us than this present moment, when chance and freedom are at work together under the guidance of a gentle and powerful Hand.

Still I may try to sum up my thoughts, and to give them a measure of unity. I may try to see whether there is at present any truth in my hypothesis that the various crises of Christ are deeply alike in their meaning; whether behind all those various conditions and circumstances, those metamorphoses of mind and speech, there is not forever the same agony of Jesus Christ, the same dismemberment. While the historian's mind inclines to point up contrast between different ages, and to present as strange what is ancient, philosophy strives to bring out fully the resemblance among things that differ only in appearance, the similarity of the fundamental conflicts.

We may ask ourselves the same question in regard to heresies that some physicians ask themselves about a 'disease'; whether they are not perhaps merely the different forms in which the same unbalance of humor appears at different times, in different ages, under different circumstances. We may ask ourselves especially whether our age does not differ from others merely in the scope, the subtlety, and the degree of concealment of this same peril of negation which has been threatening Christianity from the very start.

When we compare the various crises we gain the impression that the course of history moves in a spiral; the same rhythms appear in a more concentrated form. The crisis of the Reformation shows certain rhythms of the Arian crisis in more dramatic fashion, and with deeper roots in the consciences of men. The crisis of Europe of the last two centuries—and specially of the last two decades—recapitulates several earlier crises in greater depth, with greater scope, and with greater dangers.

I said that theological disputes seem to modern man often no more than idle talk. This is because we do not take the trouble to translate those problems into our language and to seek out their correspondences and equivalences. 'All is always alike,' said Leibniz, 'except in degrees of perfection.'

Christianity poses only one single problem, symbolized in the sibylline fish of the catacombs whose letters spell out the initials of the motto: Jesus-Christ-God's-Son-Savior. The difficulties of the mind in accepting this mystery remain much the same, in spite of all the differences in time, mentality, or expression.

The sum of religious history is the tale of a storm on the lake: catastrophe is forever possible, likely, even imminent; salvation is forever unlikely, it hangs by a thread, it depends on a combination of accidents. Every 'great heresy' always seems to

The New Dismemberment

have the greater chance on its side; and yet it passes. If it does last, it is without vigor. The frail ship of the Church does not founder.

When the human intelligence is placed face to face with the essential MYSTERY it vacillates, as I have said, from one extreme to the other. It exalts God or the Christ-God beyond the reach of knowledge. In the same breath it reduces the sense of mystery, or its moral demands, as though it meant to replace the synthesis and the sacrifice by a mixture of intransigence and compromise. The Church of Rome is not, of course, exempt from oscillations: we notice that the maximisation of one element may often be counterbalanced by the minimisation of another. Thus the affirmation of an ideal, called *thesis*, is counterbalanced by extreme flexibility in tolerating abuse or accepting a situation such as it is. This flexibility is called the *hypothesis*. Contraries oppose each other even within the Church—we have seen it, and shall always see it. But the dismemberment is never carried to the extreme. To use a simile from nuclear physics: the Catholic atom maintains its electrons in their courses: they are not *disintegrated*. They resist the bombardment of neutrons that would throw them into different orbits and join them in the composition of strange structures.

In this, I believe, resides the historical and philosophical originality of *structure* and *development*, of this temporal essence called Catholicism. With Newman, I see here an eternal Idea cast into the world of time.

In such an essence which would tend to fall apart because of all the dissolving forces within and without, there exists a bond of stability. In spite of the obscurity of the faith, the balance of complementary truths is kept.

But if we would understand the difficulty, the rareness, the price and, I dare say, the splendor of this synthesis, the study of the great choices is of high value. Without it the synthesis might seem to be a fact of nature or of chance, something that goes without saying—as health is for those who have never been ill.

Catholicism demands an effort to go from the periphery of the truths to their core, their heart which is the fountain-head. This is the road I have tried to trace here; where I have criticized I meant to be respectful and constructive. And to those whom I

181

criticized I would say the words of St Augustine, so profound and so simple: 'If I oppose you, it is to give you the fulness.' *Tibi contradico ut totum possideas.*

It is a way of sorrows, this road to unity, a way that truly dismembers. But it is a way that converges and that, like every way of sorrows, unites us with our fellows, with ourselves, and with God.

I am surprised no longer that in our day we see within each of the spiritual families, within each of the Christian confessions, the rise of men who do not think it impossible to conceive of a new 'recapitulation in Christ' of what has been wrenched apart; provided each one will agree to distinguish within his own faith what is essential from what is not. Could it be that for the first time we have reached a moment in history when the reunification of the disjointed members is not just a dream? That the distance between the disjointed Churches and the Church is not un-bridgeable? Infinitely small distances of this kind are no doubt the hardest to reduce, for all the infinity of the difference is in them compressed. Once the tie of love has been untied, the last steps are the steps which are never taken.

When all things will be one—and they will be one, tomorrow, tonight, in the other world—when all the differences, divergences, and failures will have disappeared, we shall understand that 'for those who love God everything works for the good'. What to Catholics looks like a failure is to have separated from the bond of unity at the highest point: in short not to have imitated Paul in his attitude toward Peter. The end of the *era of heresies* will be symbolized by the accord of Paul and Peter, which is the bond of the universal Church. There would then be left only the apocalyptic battle: on the one side the partisans of Nothingness, and on the other the partisans of Being gathered round the sons of Abraham, in the line of descent from which Christ has sprung and which the Church continues on this earth.

I look back one last time on what I have written. If I were to sum it up in a word, I would say that I have studied one by one —and more secretly, all together—the great partial choices that mark the history of man through twenty centuries; a short span of time, perhaps.

The New Dismemberment

In each of these great choices I have found, I think, a part that negates and a part that affirms. The affirmations are converging, I believe, and once they are detached from the negations are capable of joining in a richer Unity. The negations often seemed to me in conflict among themselves, and to blot each other out. Their dark outlines then make us aware of a core that sheds a dark light—the true mystery, the abode of the All, which we still see dimly, until we see face to face. If every little fragment of the Total Truth, exalted by an exclusive choice, is so entrancing, how much more entrancing will be all the fragments united in the All.

Index

Index

Index

Hermeticism, 53
Hilary, 87
Hildebert, 127
Hobbes, Thomas, 148
homoousios, 84-5, 86, 92
Hugo, Victor, 102, 104
Hume, David, 148
Hutin, Serge, 53

Innocent III, and the Albigensians, 126, 128-9, 138
Inquisition, the, 130
Irenaeus, St, 45, 57
Islam, definition of, 29; speed and extent of its conquests, 99, 105, 108; success of its primitive simplification, 100, 105, 111; compared with Arianism, 101; Mohammed and the Koran, 101-3; a path between Christianity and paganism, 103; its morality, 103-4, 111-12; war the sacral act, 104-5; superiority in the sciences, 105-6; contact with Greek culture, 106-7; influence on Western culture, 107-8; its lasting qualities and impenetrability, 22, 108, 110-12; relations with Judaism, 108-9; immune to Christian mission, 109-10; success in Africa, 110; modern contacts—anti-Christian and antiatheist, 112-13; the possible conflict with communism, 113-14, 116; a possible link between Judaism and Christianity, 114-17
Ismaelites, 53
Israeli, Isaac, 107

James, St, 41, 44
Jerusalem, Council of, 35-7; sack by the Romans, 44; falls to the Muslims, 105
Joachim of Flora, 125
John XXIII, 29-30

John, King of England, 129
Joubert, 89
Judaism: the first crisis in the Church, 19-20; the heritage of Israel conflicts with the new essentials, 33-5; the Council of Jerusalem, 35-7; the foresight of St Paul, 36-8; if Paul had not lived, 40-1; the old and the new in the Church, 41-2; if the separation had not come about, 42-3; Jewish mysticism, 43-4; 'His own received him not', 44; extinction or exile of Jewish Christians, 44-5; Judeo-Christian theology, 46-7
Judeo-Christians, definition of, 28
Jung, C. G., 53, 74

Ka'ba, the, 101
Kabbalah, the, 53
Kant, Immanuel, 148, 162
Khadijah, 102
Kindi, 107
Koran, the, 101-4

Laity, the, after Montanism, 71
Lammenais, 66
Lavaud, 134
Leibniz, 154, 162, 178, 180
Leonard, A., 53
Liberius, Pope, 87, 88
Livermann, Father, 110
Locke, John, 148
Luther, Martin, 14, 29, 146, 150

Maimonides, 107
Malebranche, 162
Manichaeism, 53, 54
Marcion, 20, 28, 51; on the human condition, 62; sees Jesus as a religious myth, 66-8; his effect on the Church, 68-9

Index

Sardica, 86
Sartre, J.-P., 57
Schism, definition of, 27
Scripture, established after Marcion, 68
Seleucia, 'Council' of, 86
Siegfried, André, 11, 43
Simon de Montfort, 129
Simon Magus, 51
Sirmium, 'Council' of, 86
Solobiev, 75
Spain, falls to the Muslims, 105
Spinoza, 56
Stephen, St, 37
Surrealism, 52, 53, 75

Tarik, 105
Tertullian, 28, 70-1
Theodoret, 89
Theosophy, 52, 53, 75

Tillich, Paul, 156
Toulouse, Albigensian council at, 126
Toumliline, monastery of, 110
Tours, Council of, 126
Toynbee, Arnold J., 11
Tradition, strengthened after Marcion, 68-9
Trent, Council of, 29

Valentinus, 28, 51; his system of gnosticism, 58-60; on the human condition, 62
Vatican Council (1870), 175; (1962), 29-30, 168
Vogel, Mlle C. de, on the Protestant attitude, 158-60

Waldo, Peter, 125
William of Paris, 125